Leadership

Biblical Truth for a New Generation of Leaders

FRANK P. ADAMS

Published by: King's Way Publishing
A division of King's Way Enterprises, Inc.
27 Dawson Drive, Fredericksburg, VA. 22405

ISBN: 978-0692363096 (King's Way Publishing)
ISBN 13: 0692363092

DEDICATION

This book is dedicated to my wife Brenda. Honey, thanks for believing in me and sticking with me all these years. Your love and commitment to me and the service of Jesus Christ is an anchor in my life. Thanks for everything. I mean everything! You have been by my side for over four decades. You are a great wife and mother. Your love has warmed our home and blessed everyone who had the opportunity to share in it.

I look forward to the years we will have together in the service of Christ. We have shared the labor and love of ministry and we will each wear the crown at Christ coming.

CONTENTS

Introduction

The Call of God   14

Five Leadership Essentials   18

A Good Leader   22

A Leader Worth Following   26

The Work of Ministry   30

Getting a Handle on Leadership   33

How God Directs His Work   37

Keys to Organizational Success   41

Team Building   45

Seeing What Has Never Been Seen   49

Don't Put God in a Box   53

Risk Takers   56

The "IT" Factor   59

Don't Shoot Yourself in the Foot   63

Preparing for Increase   67

Unlock Your Future   71

Maintaining Your Spiritual Edge   75

How to Break a Drought   80

Moving Forward   84

A Winning Team   87

The Ministry of Maturity   91

Multiplication Follows Consecration   94

Wise Council   97

Be Strong and Do It   100

The Man of God   104

The Generosity of God   107

The Gift of Sight   110

Take the Lead   113

Christ's Final Instructions   116

The Lord of Heaven's Armies   119

Stop Worrying—Start Believing   122

The God Who Hides Himself   125

Hopeless Without the Spirit   128

The Wind of the Spirit   131

The Church and the Gospel   134

God Exceeds the Need   137

When God Turns Up the Heat   140

The Power of the Tithe   143

Money Follows Vision   146

Be There   149

Money for Ministry   152

The Buy In   155

How to "Vet" a Potential Leader   158

God Is in the Details   161

The Place of Blessing   164

The Leader as Messenger   167

The Authentic Minister   169

Ministry Is a Work of Faith   171

The Spirit of the Taker   174

The Ministry of Illumination   177

Closing the Door on the Devil   180

A Mouth Filled with Laughter   183

Jesus Is a People Person   186

Open Your Mouth Wide   189

Against the Odds   192

A Model Leader   195

Rules of Engagement   198

When Christ Is in the House   201

The Spirit of the House   204

Preparation for Visitation   207

The Sacrifice of Praise   210

The Unchanging Christ   213

When You're in a Hurry and God Isn't   216

The Mind of a Champion   219

The Blessing of Good Leadership   221

The Acts 2 Church   224

Try Again   227

"Naivete" Hurts the Church   229

How Long Are You Going to Wait?   232

Going Public with Your Faith   235

What Faith in God Will Do   238

A Leader's Resolve   241

Introduction

"All scripture is given by inspiration of God, and is profitable for doctrine, for reproof, for correction, for instruction in righteousness, that the man of God may be thoroughly equipped for every good work." 2Timothy 3:16–17 NKJ

Leadership Has a Voice

When John the Baptist was asked to identify himself, he responded, "I am a voice of one crying in the wilderness; 'make straight the way of the Lord.'" John 1:23 NKJ

Leaders are given a voice, and their voice is a voice of influence. Leaders are not to be silent. They are the voice of the Lord. When leaders speak from God's word, good things happen. When leaders are silent or speak from a source other than God's word, leadership influence is diminished. God's word in the leader's mouth prepares the leader for service.

"Then the lord put forth his hand and touched my mouth, and the lord said to me: 'Behold, I have put my words in your mouth.'" Jeremiah 1:9 NKJ

God's Promise to Leaders

In 2 Timothy 3:16–17 God makes a promise to his leaders that no human author can make. No other book can be compared to the Bible when it comes to leadership. The Bible is the only "divinely inspired" book on leadership. When a leader's mouth is filled with God's word, the church is filled with God's power.

The Bible promises to thoroughly equip leaders for every good work. To "thoroughly equip" is a term with reference to a large ship preparing for a voyage. The ship is said to be "thoroughly equipped" when every resource for a successful journey has been anticipated and placed on board in advance. No book other than the Bible can make that promise to a leader.

The Bible provides the leader with the resources required to be profitable and to accurately instruct the church in life, leadership, and mission. The Bible will reveal wrong belief leading to wrong behavior and correct the behavior with right instruction. Only "divine inspiration" can so thoroughly equip for leadership. The word of God alone will equip the church for every good work.

These leadership lessons are sent forth with the prayer that they will be used to raise the level of leadership in God's church. I recommend that pastors/leaders adapt the lessons for use with their staff, boards, deacons, and lay leaders. The word of God is the voice of leadership. When leaders speak the word of God into the lives of their leaders, the level of leadership will rise and the church will increase in effectiveness.

Frank Adams
Fredericksburg, VA
January 13, 2015

1

The Call of God
Mark 1:14–20

Every Christian has received a call from God. "God is faithful, by whom you were called into the fellowship of His Son, Jesus Christ our Lord" (1 Cor 1:9).

From our text we see four elements contained in the Christian's calling.

1. THE CALL TO FAITH. 1:15

> "The time is fulfilled, and the kingdom of God is at hand. Repent, and believe in the gospel" (1:15).

The call of God is a call to faith expressed in repentance, which is turning from sin to Jesus Christ. "Repent and believe the gospel" is the message of Jesus Christ and all true ministers of the gospel.

"Let us ask ourselves what we know of repentance and faith. Have we felt our sins and forsaken them? Have we laid hold of Christ and believed? We may reach Heaven without learning, or riches, or health, or worldly greatness, but we will never reach Heaven, if we die impenitent and unbelieving." (**J.C. Ryle**, *Expository Thoughts on the Gospels*)

The call to faith expressed by repentance is a call for radical heart transformation. There is urgency in Christ's call to repent and believe. The urgency is that judgment is coming.

> "Truly, these times of ignorance God overlooked, but now commands all men everywhere to repent, because He has appointed a day on which He will judge the world in righteousness by the man whom He has ordained. He has given assurance of this to all by raising Him from the dead." (Acts 17:30–31)

2. THE CALL TO FOLLOW. 1:16–18

A call to follow Christ is a call to be with Christ, to know him, to fellowship with him: to learn of him and ultimately to become like him. "It is enough for a disciple that he be like his teacher…" (Mt 10:25). A call to follow Christ is a call to live one's life in pursuit of Christ.

"There are those so hungry, so desperate for His presence, that they become consumed with finding Him." (**Tommy Tenney**, *The God Chasers*)

To "follow" is the word of Christian discipleship. All four gospel writers use it in a sense of a commitment that breaks all other ties (Mt 10:37). The first disciples "forsook all and followed Him." It was their calling and is our calling.

3. THE CALL TO FISH. 1:17

> "Follow Me, and I will make you become fishers of men" (1:17).

Following Christ is never just about "Jesus and me." Every follower is to be a fisher of men. It is not by accident that the best known symbol of Christianity is a fish.

"Millions of surveys which we have helped to take around the world indicate that approximately **98** percent of Christians do not regularly introduce others to the savior." (**Bill Bright**, *Campus Crusade)*

"The late Sam Shoemaker, an Episcopalian Bishop, summed up the situation this way: 'In the great commission the Lord has called us to be—like Peter—fishers of men. We've turned the commission around so that we have become merely keepers of the aquarium. Occasionally I take some fish out of your bowl and put them into mine, and you do the same with my bowl. But we're all tending the same fish.'" (**E.M. Griffin**, *The Mind Changers*)

4. A CALL TO FIX. 1:19–20

> "...He saw James, the son of Zebedee, and John his brother, who also were in the boat mending their nets*"* (1:19).

The word "mending" means to fix what is broken. It has the idea of: to repair, restore, and return to service. Mending is the word for "perfecting" or "equipping" the saints (Eph 4:12). That which was damaged is healed and returned to rightful order and usefulness.

The church is a healing and restoring community, a place where broken people are restored to God's original intent and design for their lives. What John and his brother were doing with the nets, the church does for people.

In the words of John Newton: "I am not what I might be, I am not what I ought to be, and I am not what I wish to be. I am not what I hope to be, but I thank God I am not what I once was, and I can say with the great apostle, 'By the grace of God, I am what I am.'"

These four callings are fundamental and foundational to all future callings in our life. Before we are called to any other calling, or more specific calling of service, we are called to faith, we are called to follow, to fish, and to fix. "You see your calling, brethren" (1 Cor 1:26).

2

Five Leadership Essentials

The word essential means that which is fundamental or indispensable, basic and necessary, all-important and critical.

1. FELLOWSHIP, THE WAITING OF A LEADER

> "Now when Moses went into the tabernacle of the meeting to speak with Him, he heard the voice of One speaking to him from above the mercy seat that was the ark of the testimony, from between the two cherubim; thus he spoke unto him." (Numbers 7:89)

Moses separated himself from the people and went to the place where God could be found. Moses went to the right place, got in the right posture, and had the right disposition, a listening heart.

Fellowship with God is essential to effective leadership. Leaders lead from their fellowship with Jesus. What a leader is in private with Jesus is what a leader is in public with people. The church must have leaders who have been with Jesus (Acts 4:13). A leader can't tell you how to get where he has never been. The church must warm herself by the fire that warms the leader's heart. What fires the leader's heart will catch fire in the people's heart.

2. FOLLOWSHIP, THE WALK OF THE LEADER

> "If any one serves Me, let him follow Me; and where I am, there my servant will be also. If anyone serves Me, him my father will honor" (Jn 12:26).

S.I. McMillen, in his book *None of These Diseases*, tells the story of a young woman who wanted to go to college. Her heart sank when she read the question on the application form that asked, "Are you a leader?" Being both honest and conscientious, she wrote "no." She returned the application and expected the worst, but to her surprise she received a letter from the college: "Dear Applicant, a study of the application forms reveals that this year our college will have 1,452 leaders. We are accepting you because we feel it is imperative that they have at least one follower."

Before we become a leader, we must be a follower. A follower of Jesus Christ and those other leaders we have before us.

"Those who follow Christ have three distinct marks: they look only in one direction, they can never turn back, they no longer have plans of their own." **(A.W. Tozer)**

3. STEWARDSHIP, THE WORK OF THE LEADER

> "Let a man so consider us, as servants of Christ and stewards of the mysteries of God" (1 Cor 4:1).

Stewards manage the assets of another. Stewards are to be both faithful and fruitful. The faithful, fruitful steward is rewarded, unlike the lazy, slothful servant (Mt 25:14–30). What has been given must be used and increased.

"Faithfulness is accomplishing as much as possible with the

resources and talents God has given us. God doesn't expect us to produce more than we can, but he does expect us to produce all that we can by his power within us. Ministry must be both faithful and fruitful." (**Rick Warren**)

4. LORDSHIP, THE WORSHIP OF THE LEADER

The word "Lord" signifies owner, master, one who has absolute dominion, supreme authority, unlimited power arising from ownership. It involves total submission on our parts to God's will, not out of slavish fear, but joyfully and willingly. (Hayford Bible Handbook)

Leaders model lordship. They demonstrate what it means to live out the lordship of Jesus Christ in everyday life.

"Jesus Christ is not valued at all until he is valued above all." (**Augustine**)

> "I beseech you therefore, brethren, by the mercies of God, that you present your bodies a living sacrifice, which is your reasonable service." (Rom 12:1)

"Reasonable service" is translated your "spiritual worship" in the revised version.

5. CHAMPIONSHIP, THE WILL OF THE LEADER

The will of the champion overcomes obstacles to finish well. It is not where you start that is important, but where you finish.

"The Greeks had a race in their Olympic games that was unique. The winner was not the runner who finished first; it was the runner who finished first with his torch still lit. I want to run all the way with the flame of my torch still lit for Him." (**J. Stowell,** *Fan the Flame*)

"Let us run with endurance the race that is set before us" (Heb 12:1).

Leaders are champions who run the race of eternal life with their torch lit. Lighting the way through the darkness for others to follow.

3

A Good Leader
2 Samuel 5:1–5, 9–20

Good leadership is essential to the success of any organization. Wherever an organization finds itself—it is there as a result of its leadership. Wherever an organization is in the future, it will be the result of leadership. You can't separate the success of an organization from its leadership. An organization without good leadership is destined to fail. Securing good leaders will assure the success of an organization. There is no problem that can't be solved with good leaders.

1. A GOOD LEADER IS SELECTED FROM AMONG THE PEOPLE. 5:1

Then all the tribes of Israel came to David at Hebron and spoke, saying, "Indeed we are your bone and your flesh" (5:1).

Israel selected David to lead them because he was one of them. The apostles instructed the infant church: "Therefore, brethren, seek out from among you seven men…" (Acts 6:3). A good leader is one who is raised up from the people they are to lead.

Good leadership begins with good selection. The first apostles selected men of good reputation, filled with the Holy Spirit and wisdom (Acts 6:3). As a result, the word of God increased and the number of disciples multiplied. The best leaders are home-grown. Raised up in the midst of those they are to serve. This gives those selected instant credibility among those they are to lead.

2. A GOOD LEADER HAS SERVED AS A GOOD SUBORDINATE. 5:2

> "Also, in time past, when Saul was king over us, you were the one who led Israel out and brought them in; and the Lord said to you 'You shall shepherd My people Israel, and be ruler over Israel'" (5:2).

A good leader has served others successfully. (See Lk 16:10–13.) David served as Saul's subordinate before he became king. Faithfulness in another's ministry prepares you for your own ministry of leadership. Joshua served Moses, Elisha poured water on the hands of Elijah, and Timothy served Paul as a son with his father. Any potential leader must be willing to work and make another successful before leading their own ministry.

3. A GOOD LEADER HAS A CLEAR CALL FROM GOD. 5:2b

> "The Lord said to you, you shall shepherd My people Israel, and be ruler over Israel" (5:2b).

A clear call from God is essential to being a good leader. "No man takes this honor to himself, but he who is called by God, just as Aaron was" (Heb 5:4). It is important that the leader be convinced of the call to lead God's people. Leadership is a calling, not a career choice. All the tribes of Israel who had gathered at Hebron to anoint David as king recognized and confirmed David's call to lead Israel.

Along with the clear call from God to lead comes the anointing of God that enables the leader to lead successfully (5:3).

4. A GOOD LEADER HAS THE SUPPORT OF OTHER LEADERS. 5:3

"Therefore all the elders of Israel came to the king at Hebron, and King David made a covenant with them at Hebron before the Lord, and they anointed David king over Israel" (5:3).

The elders recognized David's appointment and anointing to be king. There were many leaders in Israel, but only one king. All the leaders recognized and accepted David's leadership. Israel had numerous leaders who served in various levels of leadership. All the leaders of Israel made a covenant with David and supported his leadership. Good leadership must seek and secure the support and cooperation of other leaders for there to be success.

5. A GOOD LEADER'S INFLUENCE INCREASES WITH TIME. 5:10

"So David went on and became great, and the Lord God of hosts was with him" (5:10).

Leaders lead initially from their "position" as leader. With time, they become a "person" of influence and lead from who they are among the people rather than from the position they hold. This can be the difference between success and significance.

The success of the leader translates to the success of the organization. The leader and those they lead rise together. David's greatness became Israel's greatness. The success of the organization is tied to its leadership. An organization will rise only as high as the leaders who lead.

> "So David knew that the Lord had established him as king over Israel, and that He had exalted his kingdom for the sake of His people Israel" (5:12).

6. GOOD LEADERS LEAD TO VICTORY. 5:19–20

> "And the Lord said to David, 'Go up, for I will doubtless deliver the Philistines into your hand.' So David went to Baal Perazim, and David defeated them there…" (5:19–20).

Good leaders lead to victory. David led Israel to victory against the Philistines. "Saul has slain his thousands and David his ten thousands" (1 Sam 18:7). Good leaders solve organizational problems. Good leaders lead their people to victory. A single victory at the opportune time will give way to multiple victories for the people. Good leaders have solutions. People look to leaders to create victory opportunities—good leaders become heroes of the people they lead.

4

A Leader Worth Following
Psalm 78:72

"So he shepherded them according to the integrity of his heart and guided them by the skillfulness of his hands" (78:72).

David was a leader worth following. To shepherd is to lead. A shepherd/leader goes before the sheep and the sheep follow. Shepherds/leaders guide sheep, they don't drive them. Sheep will scatter if driven. Shepherds/leaders know their sheep and the sheep know their leader and follow. A leader must be follow-able. Not all leaders are worthy of followers.

1. A LEADER WORTH FOLLOWING HAS CHARACTER (INTEGRITY).

"So he shepherded them according to the integrity of his heart..." (78:72).

"Character is <u>NOT</u> essential to leadership," says **Andy Stanley,** in his book *The Next Generation Leader*. "We all know leaders who have led large organizations and garnered the loyalty of many followers, and yet lacked character; however, character is what makes a leader worth following."

Character is an issue of the heart. Leaders live by higher standards than followers. The higher you rise in leadership, the fewer rights you have and the more character is required. Character enables leaders to shepherd people for their best interest rather than the leader's interest. The latter is manipulation, the former motivation.

"Image is what people think we are, integrity is what we really are." **(John Maxwell,** *Developing the Leader Within*)

Character or integrity is what we are when alone and no one is observing. David led by the integrity of his heart. A leader worth following has character.

"Character may manifest in the great moments, but it is made in the small ones." **(Phillips Brooks)**

"The best index to a person's character is (a) how he treats people who can't do him any good, and (b) how he treats people who can't fight back." **(Abigail Van Buren)**

2. A LEADER WORTH FOLLOWING IS COMPETENT (SKILLFUL).

"And guided them by the skillfulness of his hands" (78:72).

Skill is essential to leadership. Leadership skills can be learned. There is no substitute for skill. A doctor may have a great bedside manner with a patient, but what is most significant is the physician's skill. Leaders must acquire skills essential to leadership. Without the basic skills, good intentions won't take you very far.

"Most of the worst managerial calamities we caused—ones in which people got deeply hurt—can be traced back to my leaning overly optimistically to put people in a role they were ill equipped for." (**Bill Hybles,** *Ax*i*om*)

3. A LEADER WORTH FOLLOWING HAS THE COOPERATION OF PEOPLE.

"So he shepherded them…" (78:72).

"Few people are successful unless a lot of people want them to be." (**John Maxwell,** *Leadership Gold*)

This is the law of "the buy-in." People must "buy-in" to the leader before they "buy-in" to his vision. The character of the leader justifies the "buy-in." Leaders have followers. Jesus's disciples bought in to him, before they ever knew the details of his mission.

"Follow me…"

"The most powerful two-word leadership phrase Jesus ever uttered was "Follow me." The apostle Paul called believers to imitate him just as he imitated Christ. Follow me, imitate me—both statements refer to the power of leading by example.

If you cannot say, "Follow me" to your followers—and mean it—then you've got a problem. A big one. Follow my values. Follow my integrity. Follow my work ethic, my commitment, and my communication patterns. Fight as I fight. Focus as I focus. Sacrifice as I sacrifice. Love as I love. Repent as I repent. Admit wrong as I admit wrong. Endure hardship as I endure hardship. When requisite actions back them up, these are the words that set followers' hearts soaring." (**Bill Hybels,** *Ax*i*om*)

Leadership in the church is selected based first and foremost on character and competency. Character and competency are twin towers of leadership. A good person doing a terrible job does not advance Christ's cause. Character needs to be coupled with competency for results.

> "Therefore, brethren, seek out from among you seven men of good reputation, full of the Holy Spirit and wisdom, whom we may appoint over this business" (Acts 6:3).

5

The Work of Ministry
Ephesians 4:12

"For the equipping of the saints for the work of the ministry, for edifying of the body of Christ" (4:12).

All believers are to be employed in the work of ministry. Leaders equip others for work in ministry (4:11–12). Believers have been graced and gifted for ministry (Eph 4:7–8; 1 Pet 4:10–11).

1. THE WORK OF THE MINISTRY IS REAL WORK.

The word for work in our text is ERON: meaning to work, to toil, an effort, act, deed, or labor. Jesus established a culture of sacrifice and service in His church. (Jn 13:2–17). The work of the ministry flourishes when the people have a mind to work (Neh 4:6).

"The laity are not passengers on a cruise ship—they are the crew." **(Elton Trueblood)**

The work of the ministry is real work, often hard work (Phil 2:17). The more people involved in the work of ministry, the stronger and healthier the church becomes.

Membership without ministry must be unacceptable and avoided. Granting rights and privileges without responsibility turns one into a liability rather than an asset. A member who "consumes" only will eventually become the church's worst critic. You value only what you personally invest in.

The best opportunity to connect membership with ministry is when people first come for membership. There will never be a time when people are more open to ministry involvement than when coming for membership. They are new to the church and want to be involved. There are two basic reasons people stay with a congregation, relationship and responsibilities. When these are available, they generally stay.

Christians have been called to "active duty." An "inactive Christian" is an oxymoron. "Who gave Himself for us that He might redeem us from every lawless deed and purify for Himself His own special people, zealous for good works. Speak these things, exhort, and rebuke with all authority, let no one despise you" (Tit 2:14–15).

2. THE WORK OF THE MINISTRY IS REASONABLE WORK.

> "I beseech you therefore, brethren, by the mercies of God, that you present your bodies a living sacrifice, holy, acceptable to God, which is your reasonable service" (Rom 12:1).

"Reasonable Service" is logical ministry. Sacrifice in service for Christ is not unreasonable or illogical. The work of the ministry is reasonable. It calls for presenting one's self as a living sacrifice to God.

To call God's people to sacrifice is not unreasonable. What is unreasonable is when 80 percent of the church leaves 20 percent of His people to do 100 percent of the work. Any industry would collapse with that margin of effectiveness. The church grows when each part does its share of the work of ministry (Eph 4:16).

"Most people wish to serve God—but in an advisory capacity only." (**Author Unknown**)

"There are three kinds of workers. For example, when a piano is to be moved, the first kind gets behind and pushes, the second pulls and guides, and the third grabs the piano stool." (**Unknown**)

3. THE WORK OF THE MINISTRY IS A REWARDED WORK.

> "Each one will receive his own reward according to his labor" (1 Cor 3:8).

> "For God is not unjust to forget your work of faith and labor of love which you have shown toward his name" (Heb 6:10).

"One day in heaven will pay you, yes, overpay your blood, bonds, sorrow and suffering; it will trouble angel's understanding to lay account of that surplus glory which eternity can and will give you." (**Samuel Rutherford**)

"Earth for work, heaven for wages, this life for the battle, another for the crown, time for employment, eternity for enjoyment." (**Thomas Guthrie**)

Why were we left here, since heaven is a much better place? The fourth chapter of Ephesians gives three reasons we were left here instead of being taken immediately to heaven. We were left here for: (1) maturity (4:13); (2) for ministry (4:12); (3) for multiplication (4:16). Let's not waste the time we have remaining.

6

Getting a Handle on Leadership
Hebrews 10:24

"And let us consider one another in order to stir up love and good works" (10:24).

Leaders, specifically lay leaders, need to understand leadership as influence. When lay leaders intentionally influence others, their positive impact is felt throughout the congregation. When lay leaders fail to intentionally influence others positively, it creates a vacuum of leadership. All sorts of disturbing and hideous things develop in the vacuum.

The motive for intentionally influencing others is to provoke or stir up to love and good works. Leaders influence others on purpose—with a purpose.

"Let us" is both a command and a choice we make to intentionally impact the lives of those we lead. Leadership stirs up others to love and good works. Love speaks of how we view things—good works speak of how we do things. Leadership influences attitudes and actions.

1. LEADERS INFLUENCE VERBALLY.

Leadership has a voice. When we speak, we influence. Nothing will change until someone speaks up for change. Silence creates a leadership vacuum. In this vacuum the level of excellence diminishes to the lowest level. When leaders voice excellence, excellence will increase. Remaining silent in the presence of poor performance is to reinforce the poor performance. To speak for and model excellence is to establish excellence.

Lay leaders must be taught and encouraged to exercise leadership influence by speaking up, about, and into situations and people. This peer pressure is often more effective than pastoral pressure. Lay leaders listen to connect and speak to direct and correct.

2. LEADERS INFLUENCE VISUALLY.

Leaders lead by their example. People follow what they see in their leaders. What people have heard from their leaders, they must see in their leaders. This gives credibility to lay leaders. Positive performance by lay leaders will be repeated by those who observe their attitude and actions. All leaders—lay and otherwise—must be an example worth following (1 Tim 4:12). Actions always speak louder than words.

"Few things are harder to put up with than the annoyance of a good example." (**Mark Twain**)

3. LEADERS INFLUENCE WITH VALUES.

"Values communicate what really matters. Values say 'This is what we stand for, this is who we are, and this is what we are all about. Values can change. Values create change. Values influence behavior, inspiring action in others. Values contribute to organizational success. Values tell everyone what is important to the organization. Values set priorities and shape decision making. Values are passionate—they connect with your emotions. In order to be credible our values must be biblical." (Excerpts from *Advanced Strategic Planning*, by **Aubrey Malphors**)

"What we obtain too cheap, we esteem too lightly…it is dearness only that gives everything its value." (**Unknown**)

Values must mean something and lead to something. Values held that don't result in action are merely sentiments, not values. Values impact the heart and not just the head.

"At one time, Francis Schaeffer says, he shared a platform with former cabinet member and urban leader John Gardner, during which Gardner spoke on the need to restore values to our culture. After he finished, a Harvard student asked him: 'On what do you build your values?' Gardner, usually articulate and erudite, paused, looked down, and said, 'I do not know.' I repeatedly encounter the same reaction. When I have contended before scholars and college audiences that in a secular, relativistic society there is no basis for ethics, no one has ever challenged me. In fact, in private they often agree." (**Charles W. Colson,** *The Body*)

4. LEADERS INFLUENCE WITH VISION.

Vision is about tomorrow. Vision is about what could be, what should be, what must be, and not about what has been. Vision is about the future; it is about tomorrow, which impacts today.

When Helen Keller was asked what would be worse than being born blind, she quickly replied, "To have sight and no vision." A vision of the future is essential to leadership. Leaders influence others toward a vision of the future. With vision we are able to see the future and seize the future.

With a vision the church will thrive; without a vision the church will die (Prov 29:18).

"Vision: the capacity to create a compelling picture of the desired state of affairs that inspires people to respond; that which is desirable, which could be, should be; that which is attainable. A godly vision is right for the times, right for the church, and right for the people. A godly vision promotes faith rather than fear. A godly vision motivates people to action. A godly vision requires risk-taking. A godly vision glorifies God, not people." (**Bob Logan**)

Lay leadership is critical to the success of the local church. Lay leaders must be equipped to impact the lives of those who look for their leadership. Leadership is the exercise of influence, and we must influence others intentionally, on purpose, and with purpose.

> "And let us consider one another in order to stir up love and good works" (Heb 10:24).

7

How God Directs His Work
Ecclesiastes 3:1–22

In the third chapter of Ecclesiastes, there are five principles by which God directs His work.

1. THERE IS A GOD-GIVEN TASK.

> "I have seen the God-given task with which the sons of men are to be occupied" (Eccl 3:10).

A task is a divine assignment. We are to be occupied with the task God has assigned. The word occupied ("exercised," KJV) means to bestow labor, to work, to till, to bring forth fruit.

In seeking to discover one's assigned task, two things should be considered: one's giftedness and one's irritants. One's gift determines and defines one's calling (1 Pt 4:10–11). What most irritates may be your assignment. What bothers you most may be your assigned task to correct.

"This may strike you as odd or unorthodox to hear it phrased this way, but I believe frustration is a major precursor and indication of vision. If you're not sure what God has ordained your ministry to be, perhaps you should begin by asking yourself, what frustrates me?" (**Robert Morris**, *The Blessed Church*)

2. THERE IS A GOD-GIVEN TIME.

> "To everything there is a season, a time for every purpose under heaven" (Eccl 3:1).

Wisdom waits for God's seasons and times. When we wait for God, we work with him rather than for him. "For since the beginning of the world men have not heard nor perceived by the ear, nor has the eye seen any God besides you, who acts for the one who waits for Him" (Is 64:4).

"A key responsibility of the leader is to know what season the organization is in, to name it, and then communicate the implications of that season for his followers." (**Bill Hybels,** *Ax*i*om)*

3. THERE IS A GOD-GIVEN TESTIMONY.

> "He has made everything beautiful in its time...I know that whatever God does, it shall be forever. Nothing can be added to it and nothing taken from it. God does it that men should fear before Him...God requires an accounting of what is past" (Eccl 3:11, 14–15).

The testimony that is given concerning one's assigned task is: (1) God's work is beautiful; (2) God's work is eternal; (3) Man by his own effort can neither add to or take from God's work; (4) Man is accountable to God for his work; (5) Those who work for God should fear Him.

One's work is either wood, hay, or stubble. When it is wood, hay, or stubble, the worker will suffer the loss of his labor. When one's work is gold, silver, and precious stone, the worker's labor will survive the fire of God's scrutiny and the worker will be rewarded (1 Cor 3:12).

4. THERE IS A GOD-GIVEN TEMPERAMENT.

> "I know that nothing is better for them than to rejoice, and to do good in their lives, and also that every man should eat and drink and enjoy the good of all his labor—it is the gift of God" (Eccl 3:12–13).

"Temperament" can be defined as one's frame of mind, inner disposition, or attitude. The proper temperament for God's work is:

- Rejoice in it
- Do good in it
- Enjoy it
- Be grateful for it

Good temperament (attitude) will assure the success of almost any endeavor. A chaplain was speaking to a soldier lying on a cot in an army hospital: "You have lost your arm in the great cause," he said. "No," said the soldier with a smile. "I didn't lose it—I gave it." One's temperament in any situation is a choice. We choose the attitude we will live our lives with.

"Everything can be taken from a man but one thing—to choose one's attitude in any given set of circumstances, to choose one's way." (**Victor Frankl**, Concentration Camp Survivor)

5. THERE IS A GOD-GIVEN TEST.

> "I said in my heart, concerning the condition of the sons of men, God tests them, that they may see that they themselves are like animals" (Eccl 3:18).

God tests the sons of men! Every work will be tested (1 Cor 3:13–15). Every thought, intent, and motive of the heart is tested (Prov 20:27). God "tests" for diagnosis and development. Satan "tempts" for discouragement, distraction, and destruction. God tests in order to approve and advance his work and workers. When a worker and a work are tested and passed, promotion and increased opportunities follow. God tests to purge, polish, promote, and to profit.

"In adversity we usually want God to do a removing job when he wants to do an improving job." (**Source Unknown**)

"Vance Havner told a story about an elderly lady who was greatly disturbed by her many troubles—both real and imaginary. Finally, someone in her family tactfully told her, 'Grandma, we've done all we can for you. You'll just have to trust God for the rest.' A look of absolute despair spread over her face as she replied, 'Oh dear, has it come to that?' Havner commented, 'It always comes to that, so we might as well begin with that!' (**Vance Havner**)

8

Keys to Organizational Success

John Wooden, basketball coach of UCLA during its dynasty years, was asked the key to his success. His answer: "We master the basics, we drill over and over again on the fundamentals."

No matter how basic or advanced an organization, there are fundamentals that must be in play and remain in play to assure success. An organization never gets too successful or profitable that the fundamentals can be ignored.

1. RECRUIT RIGHT AND THINGS WILL BE RIGHT.

High expectations will attract high achievers. Hiding or minimizing the cost diminishes the value of the work and the worker. Recruiters must never hide the cost when recruiting, especially when recruiting volunteers.

2. APPRECIATION IS COMPENSATION.

Surveys reveal that workers' performance is motivated more by the show of appreciation than their compensation. Everyone seeks appreciation for a job well done. When appreciation is not properly given, the worker will be discouraged and perform poorly. "Two things people want more than sex and money and that is recognition and praise." **(Mary Kay)**

"Brains, like hearts, go where appreciated." **(Robert McNamara)**

3. WHAT GETS REWARDED GETS REPEATED.

When good performance is rewarded, the performance will be repeated. When poor performance is ignored, it will be repeated also. Good work must be rewarded and bad work corrected.

4. WHAT IS NEGLECTED FALLS APART.

> "He who is slothful in his work is brother to him who is a great destroyer" (Prov 18:9).

A house will fall from neglect. The diligent attention to detail is essential to assure success in every endeavor.

5. WHAT IS CHECKED ON GETS DONE.

Oversight will prevent things from falling through the proverbial crack. Accountability promotes responsibility. Assignment of a task must be followed up with inspection of the task. Quality is assured by oversight.

6. WHAT COUNTS GETS COUNTED.

"Not everything that counts can be counted, and not everything that can be counted counts." **(Albert Einstein)**

What counts can and should be counted. The numbers don't lie—they clarify. The numbers prevent organizational denial. How will you know how well you're doing if there is no way to measure success? What "means" success to an organization must be "measured."

"Envy is the art of counting the other fellow's blessings instead of your own." **(Hamilton Wright Mabie)**

"When I started counting my blessings, my whole life turned around." **(Willie Nelson)**

7. THE LITTLE THINGS ARE BIG.

John Rockefeller says, "The secret to success is to do the common things uncommonly well." A little leaven leavens the entire lump. The little foxes spoil the vines. Attention to the little and often overlooked details leads to bigger opportunities. (See Lk 16:10–12).

"It is better to do a thousand things 1 percent better than just one thing 1000 percent better. Excellence is made up of a thousand little things all being done well." **(Thomas J. Peters)**

8. EXPECT RESULTS.

The church is one of the few organizations that will ask people to serve with little or no expectation of seeing results. God's people are to be both faithful and fruitful. It has been said, "You may not always get what you want, but you always get what you expect." It is preferable to be a person with high expectations of people rather than to insult people's ability with low expectations of their ability and willingness to perform at peak performance.

9. MOMENTUM MOVES MOUNTAINS.

Momentum is built by celebrating small wins along the way. Don't wait to celebrate. Celebrating builds confidence and creates momentum—you must have mo to go. When momentum arrives, obstacles are overcome. If your organization has lost momentum, get it back whatever the cost.

"If you're coasting, you're either losing momentum or else you're headed downhill." **(John Welch)**

"One way to keep momentum going is to have constantly greater goals." **(Michael Korda)**

10. PEOPLE ARE YOUR GREATEST ASSET.

"We realized that our largest asset was our work force and that our growth would come from asset appreciation." **(Larry Colin,** *Colin Service Systems***)**

Alex Haley, the author of *Roots*, has a picture in his office showing a turtle sitting atop a fence. The picture is there to remind him of a lesson he learned a long time ago. "If you see a turtle on a fence post, you know he had some help."

9

Team Building

Christianity is the greatest team effort known to man. "Team Trinity" is visible throughout scripture. Father, Son, and Holy Spirit united in a single purpose: the redemption and restoration of man. The three in one work together to accomplish their purpose on the earth. Teamwork makes the dream work.

1. TEAMS ARE ABOUT PEOPLE.

"A team is a group of people working together in a sustained effort to reach a common goal." (**Source Unknown**)

The apostle Paul demonstrated three great skills in his ministry: great preaching skills, great skill in his prayers, and the skill that makes the first two skills most effective, great people skills. His people skills made his ministry a threefold cord that could not be broken. (See Col 1:9, 25,28; 1Thess 2:7–11.)

The basis of life is people and how they relate to each other. Success, fulfillment, and happiness depend on one's ability to relate to people.

Success in any endeavor, according to a Stanford Research Group, is 12.5 percent knowledge and 87.5 percent people skills.

A. Teams outperform individuals.

"In the long run, a team will outperform an individual no matter how talented the person might be." **(Dr. Elmer Towns)**

B. "Team Players" make for winning teams.

"'Team Players' sacrifice for the team's success. Without sacrifices, you'll never know your team's potential, or your own." **(Pat Riley,** *The Leader Within*)

C. "Team Players" sacrifice personal interest for team interest.

"Teamwork requires that everyone's effort flows in a single direction. Feelings of significance happen when a team's effort takes on a life of its own." **(Pat Riley,** *The Winner Within*)

2. TEAMS ARE ABOUT TRUST.

"Members of great teams trust one another on a fundamental, emotional level—they get to a point where they can be completely open with one another without filters." **(Patrick Lencion,** *Overcoming Dysfunctions of a Team*)

A. Team members must trust their team leader.

The character of the leader is essential to trust. Character brings a consistency to the leader's life, and consistency creates a safe environment where trust is created, nurtured, and grown.

B. Team leaders must trust team members.

Team members must be trusted to carry out assignments faithfully. Team members demonstrate a loyalty to team leaders and other team members.

"Confidence in an unfaithful man in times of trouble is like a bad tooth and a foot out of joint" (Prov 25:19).

C. Team members must trust each other.

"When a gifted team dedicates itself to unselfish trust—it is ready to climb." **(Pat Riley)**

3. TEAMS ARE ABOUT WINNING.

There is little difference between winning and losing. According to research, winning teams are successful three out of five times. Losing teams are successful two out of five times. On the professional bowling tour, 5 percent difference in scores separates those who make the finals and those who are cut from the tournament and go home.

A. Winning teams are always improving.

Winning teams are always striving to do better.

B. Winning teams prepare to win.

Winning is never automatic: preparation is vital to winning. Winning doesn't just happen; someone makes it happen. The willingness to prepare to win is vital to winning.

C. Winning teams are committed.

Winning teams are not always more talented, but they are always more committed. Winning teams give their best and require the best of others.

"I refuse to lower my standards to accommodate those who refuse to raise theirs." **(Steve Gamlin)**

10

Seeing What Has Never Been Seen
Mark 2:1–12

The text concludes with the words: "We never saw anything like this" (2:12 NKJ). The four men in this account reveal how the church can see what she has never seen before.

1. BE WILLING TO TEAM UP.

> "Then they came to Him, bringing a paralytic who was carried by four men" (2:3).

None of the four men could have accomplished alone what they accomplished together. Everything changed "when they came." They came together. What they did, they did together, not apart or separate—but together.

Teamwork makes the dream work. "A team is a group of people working together in a sustained effort to accomplish a common goal." (**Source Unknown**)

"As difficult as teamwork is to measure and achieve, its power cannot be denied. When people come together and set aside their individual needs for the good of the whole, they can accomplish what might have looked impossible on paper. They do this by eliminating the politics and confusion that plague most organizations. As a result, they get more done in less time and with less cost. I think that's worth a lot of effort." **(Patrick Lencioni,** *Overcoming the Five Dysfunctions of a Team*)

2. BE WILLING TO GO UP.

> "And when they could not come near Him because of the crowd, they uncovered the roof where He was..." (2:4)

These four men could not achieve their goal on the "ground level," so they took it up a level. The "roof level" is less crowded than the ground level. If you are going to see what has never been seen, you must be willing to "take it up a notch."

You must be willing to give up to go up. Give up your current level of achievement in order to reach new levels of accomplishment. There are some things you will not see on your current level. The crowd on the ground level blocked the men from achieving their purpose. You must be willing to leave the comfort of the crowded ground level for new elevations of faith. To stay with the crowd or reach for the sky—the choice is yours to make.

The Urban Dictionary defines the phrase "take it up a notch" as: digging deeper in yourself to apply more effort toward a goal.

3. BE WILLING TO MAN UP.

> "They uncovered the roof where He was. So when they had broken through, they let down the bed on which the paralytic was lying" (2:4).

To "man up" is gender neutral. It means that when faced with a difficult decision, you make it. Someone had to tear off the first shingle or, more likely, scoop up the first clump of grass and dirt to create "the breakthrough" and remove the last barrier between the team and success. Take the criticism, endure the grief, and take the heat. Do what has to be done to get the team to the goal. There are plenty of opportunities to turn back, give up, and give in. Man up! Make it happen. People are like turtles—they only make progress when they stick their neck out.

The Urban Dictionary offers the following ideas as what is involved when one "mans up:" "To be strong, take control of the situation, rise to the moment. To work through impediments and obstacles without whining. For one to be a leader, to step up to the plate when no one else will, to give it your best shot. The phrase man up is derived from the phrase "cowboy up," be tough, do what one should do." **(Urban Dictionary.com)**

"If you want your day in the sun, expect a few blisters." **(Unknown)**

Four types of people in the church:

Those who watch things happen.

Those who don't know what is happening.

Those who resist what is happening.

Those who make things happen. **(John Maxwell)**

4. BE WILLING TO FINISH UP.

> "They let down the bed on which the paralytic was lying. When Jesus saw their faith...I say to you, arise, take up your bed, and go to your house" (2:4,10).

Complete the task—fulfill the assignment—see it through to the end. Perseverance is rewarded with victory. Persevering faith enabled the men to complete their task and reach their goal. Jesus saw the persevering faith of these four men and rewarded their efforts. Mission accomplished.

Were you to ask these men, "Was it worth the effort and sacrifice?" they would undoubtedly reply, "The victory eclipses the cost." The march to victory begins with a single step of faith. That single step of faith will be seen and rewarded.

> "All were amazed and glorified God, saying, we never saw anything like this" (2:12).

The task is finished, the assignment is complete, when God receives the glory!

How Not to Take Your Team to the Playoffs
John Maxwell

1. Allow individual interest to prevail over team interest. This is a failure to call for commitment and sacrifice for team goals.

2. Allow team members to perform at less than their absolute best.

3. Have no minimal standard of performance for the team members.

11

Don't Put God in a Box
Psalm 78:32–33, 40–41; 2 Chronicles 6:4,15

There are three reasons we place things in boxes: (1) to confine them; (2) to control them; (3) to conceal them. We are tempted to put God in a box for the same reasons.

1. WHEN WE PUT GOD IN A BOX WE LIMIT HIM.

> "Yes, again and again they tempted God and limited the Holy One of Israel." (Ps 78:41).

God is infinite and cannot be limited. However, we can limit what He is able to do in our individual lives. To "limit" God is to set an arbitrary boundary by which He is restricted in His operation in one's life.

> "Now He did not do many mighty works there because of their unbelief" (Mt 13:58).

In a sermon entitled "Limiting God," Charles Spurgeon stated: "Man is always altering what God has ordained." When we limit

53

God we are altering what He has ordained.

To "limit" means to set a boundary, to establish limits, to create a border. To say to God "This far and no further." When God is confined to our self-imposed boxes, it limits what He is able to accomplish in our personal lives as well as in the church.

2. WHEN WE PUT GOD IN A BOX WE LIVE IN FUTLITY AND FEAR.

> "In spite of this they still sinned, and did not believe in His wondrous works, therefore their days were consumed in futility and their year in fear" (Ps 78:32–33).

"Futility and fear" are the results of limiting God. "Futility," according to Webster, characterizes that which fails completely or is incapable of producing results, inept, or ineffective trifling or unimportant. "Fear," according to Webster, is a feeling of anxiety and agitation caused by the presence or nearness of danger.

The will of God for His people is to live fear-free and fruitful lives. When God is limited in our lives, the result is emptiness and anxiety.

> "Have I not commanded you? Be strong and of good courage; do not be afraid, nor dismayed, for the Lord your God is with you wherever you go" (Josh 1:9).

Three times God emphasized to Joshua, "Be strong and of good courage" (1:6,7,9). The word of God is the key to success and prosperity (Josh 1:8). With the word working in our lives we will not limit God and live in futility and fear, but in success and prosperity.

3. WHEN GOD IS RELEASED FROM OUR BOX, POSSIBILITIES EXPLODE.

"Blessed be the Lord God of Israel, who fulfilled with His hands what He spoke with His mouth to my father David" (2 Chron 6:4).

When God is set free from the confinement of our box, his power is released to work miracles for his people. God becomes bigger than our problems, circumstances, and situations. No enemy or weapon formed against us will stand.

When God is out of the Box
Ephesians 3:20

God is able to <u>do</u>...what you ask or think.

God is able to do <u>all</u>...you ask or think.

God is able to do <u>above</u> all...you ask or think.

God is able to do <u>abundantly</u> above all...you ask or think.

God is able to do <u>exceedingly</u> abundantly above all...you ask or think.

Go ahead, release God from the limits of your box. He will show himself mighty on your behalf.

12

Risk Takers
Acts 10:1–11:30

It is difficult to estimate the risk Peter is being challenged to take. The elders in Jerusalem were not going to be happy that Peter had gone into the house of an unclean, uncircumcised Gentile. The news that Gentiles were being saved without first becoming proselyte Jews and succumbing to circumcision was not going to find a sympathetic hearing in Jerusalem. Peter follows through with his new assignment at great personal risk.

"People who prefer to play it safe will never know the thrill of victory. To win a victory one must be willing to risk failure." **(John Maxwell)**

"You can't discover new oceans unless you have the courage to lose sight of the shore." **(Source Unknown)**

Five Kinds of People

- Those who hear what's happening (11:1)
- Those who oppose what's happening (11:2–3)
- Those who don't know what's happening (10:23, 11:1–2)
- Those who make things happen (10:1, 11:4)
- Those who help others make things happen (11:19–26)

1. GOD CALLS HIS PEOPLE TO TAKE RISKS. (10:9–23)

"Arise therefore, go down and go with them, doubting nothing; for I have sent them" (10:20).

God calls His people to move beyond the conventional, the comfortable, and the commonplace. The risk takers are the barrier breakers and the trailblazers.

Hudson Taylor, the great man of faith who founded the China Inland Mission, integrated faith and risk. He said, "Unless there is an element of risk in our exploits for God there is no need for faith." **(Paul Bortwich,** *Leading the Way***)**

2. WHEN GOD CALLS US TO TAKE RISKS, HE WILL COMMUNICATE CLEARLY. (10:1–23)

Both Cornelius and Peter received clear communication when God called them to take a risk. Cornelius was visited by an angel. Peter fell into a trance. Peter's direction was repeated three times. Circumstances presented themselves to Peter as three men arrived from Cornelius's house. Peter still proceeded cautiously. He arranged for others to travel with him. The journey that took Cornelius's men only a short time took Peter days. He moved cautiously. Wise risk takers don't act presumptuously. Both Cornelius and Peter took risks in response to clear direction from God. Risk takers act on the word spoken by God. Peter walked on water in response to a single word—"come." That single word sustained Peter and defied the laws of science. Risk takers are not fools; they are people of faith. Faith in what God has spoken. Risk takers are usually not presumptuous.

"God is not so much concerned about what you're doing as he is with who told you to do it." **(Source Unknown)**

3. WHEN RISKS ARE TAKEN IN OBEDIENCE TO GOD'S DIRECTION THE RESULTS ARE INCREDIBLE. (10:34–48, 11:12–18)

"While Peter was still speaking these words, the Holy Spirit fell upon all those who heard the word" (10:44).

"When they heard these things they became silent; and they glorified God, saying, then God has also granted to the Gentiles repentance to life" (11:18).

The fruit of taking risks altered church history. Incredible change occurred in Peter, the elders of the Jerusalem church, and the Jewish and Gentile nations. Risk is essential to progress. The greater the risk the greater the potential for good.

"Yes, risk taking is inherently failure prone. Otherwise, it would be called "sure-thing-taking.'" **(Jim McMahon)**

"A man would do nothing, if he waited until he could do it so well that no one would find fault with what he has done." **(Cardinal Newman)**

"Go out on a limb. That's where the fruit is." **(Jimmy Carter)**

"One of the reasons why mature people stop growing and learning," says John Garner, "is that they become less and less willing to risk failure." **(Tim Hansel,** *Eating Problems for Breakfast*)

13

The "IT" Factor
Psalm 133:1–3

"The IT Factor" is that undefined quality that sets people and organizations apart.

"The it factor is more than an attractive quality, it's the hallmark of success." (**Mark Wiskup,** *The It Factor*)

The "it factor" is portrayed in our text as unity. Unity is the quality of being united in spirit, sentiment, purpose, harmony, and agreement. "Behold, how good and how pleasant it is for brethren to dwell together in unity" (133:1).

1. "IT" IS GOOD AND PLEASANT. (133:1)

Unity is pleasant to see, hear, and experience. Unity is significant in the life of God's people. (See Jn 17:20–23; Eph 4:1–6; Prov 6:16–19.)

There are four aspects included in unity being "good and pleasant." It is morally right, psychologically healthy, aesthetically pleasing, and financially prosperous.

There is a substantial difference between union and unity. Tie two cats together by their tails, throw them over a clothesline—you will have achieved union, but not unity. In unity a solidarity is achieved. There is a oneness that exists between the many. One accord becomes one mind (Phil 2:2, 2 Cor 13:11); one mouth (1 Cor 1:10); one ministry (Eph 4:12–16); one message (1 Cor 1:18; 1Jn 1:1–5).

2. "IT" IS LIKE THE PRECIOUS OIL RUNNING DOWN. (133:2)

> "It is like the precious oil upon the head, running down on the beard, the beard of Aaron, running down on the edge of his garment" (133:2).

The anointing is precious and to be highly valued by all who wish to obtain it. The anointing consecrated and empowered Aaron for ministry. (Ex 29:1–2; Lev 8:12).

The oil was placed on the head of Aaron. Jesus is the head of the church, and the anointing flows from Him to His church. (Is 61:1; Acts 10:38; 1 Jn 2:20–27; Eph 4:30; 2 Cor 1:21–22).

When unity is broken the devil gains access. "Nor give place to the devil" (Eph 4:27). To preserve unity and prevent the devil from gaining access to the church, the apostle Paul activated seven behaviors that foster unity.

Being truthful rather than deceitful (4:25). Forgiving rather than grudging (4:26) To contribute rather than to consume (4:28). Let your speech be for good, grace, and edification rather than hurt and harm (4:29). Don't allow relational sins to grieve the Holy Spirit (4:30). Put away from you bitterness, wrath, anger, loud quarreling, evil speaking, and malice (4:31). Be kind, tenderhearted, forgiving of others as Christ was to you (4:32).

3. "IT" IS THE DEW DESCENDING. (133:3a)

> "It is like the dew of Herman, descending upon the mountains of Zion" (3a).

"Dew" gives and sustains life. Dew is a metaphor for favor. "The king's wrath is like the roaring of a lion, but his favor is like dew on the grass" (Prov 19:12). Dew is quiet and gentle—without the dew, there is drought and barrenness; with dew is fruitfulness (Deut 33:13–17, 28–29).

> "I will be like dew to Israel; He shall grow like the lily, and lengthen his roots like Lebanon. His branches shall spread; His beauty shall be like an olive tree and his fragrance like Lebanon. Those who dwell under his shadow shall return; they shall be revived like grain, and grow like a vine. Their scent shall be like the wine of Lebanon" (Hosea 14:5–7).

4. "IT" IS WHERE GOD COMMANDS THE BLESSING. (133:3b)

> "For there the Lord commanded the blessing" (3b).

Where unity exists, there God commands a blessing to be released and remain. When God's direction is followed, "there" God commands a blessing (Lev 25:18–22).

> "The Lord will command the blessing on you in your storehouses and in all to which you set your hand and he will bless you in the land which the Lord your God is giving you" (Deut 28:8).

"To command" means to constitute, appoint, send, charge, set in order. In short, make it happen!

Unity is the principal key to harvest. (See Jn 17:20–21, Jn 4:35–37).

5. "IT" IS LIFE FOREVERMORE. (133:3c)

"Life forevermore" (3c).

This life is eternal life. The life that God gives. This life is the living presence of Christ in the midst of His church. "I am there in the midst of them" (Mt 18:20). Christ's presence among His people gives them the "it" factor.

A leader may aspire to have any number of items associated with his congregation, but the one essential thing you must have is Christ's living presence. Without Christ there is no life-giving presence. A church may be "lively" without life. When a people have Christ they have the "IT Factor."

14

Don't Shoot Yourself in the Foot
Proverbs 6:16–19

Self-inflicted wounds don't only hurt, they are embarrassing.

"You're bright, hardworking, ambitious…why are you not more successful? The answer might be in you…inside your personality where learned behavior and old character traits sabotage every move you try to make." **(Dr. Daniel Amen)**

Five Areas of Self-Defeating Behavior

There are five areas of self-defeating behavior listed in Proverbs 6:16–19. These evil qualities are an abomination to God.

1. ATTITUDE.

"A proud look" (6:17).

Pride is an attitude of self-sabotage that leads to destructive behavior. Pat Riley refers to this as "the disease of me." Selfishness is the number one cause of broken relationships, and selfishness thrives in the environment of pride. Pride is the soil in which all other vices thrive. Humility is the soil in which all other virtues thrive.

"Pride is the only disease that makes everyone sick, but the one who has it." **(Source Unknown)**

The scripture admonishes: "For I say, through the grace given to me, to everyone who is among you, not to think of himself more highly than he ought to think, but to think soberly, as God has dealt to each one a measure of faith" (Rom 12:3).

"Humble people don't think less of themselves, they simply think of themselves less often." **(Source Unknown)**

2. THE MIND.

"A heart that devises wicked plans..." (6:18).

"For out of the heart proceed evil thoughts..." (Mt 15:19).

Self-defeating behavior includes actions and reactions that originate within our thoughts and emotions. Self-defeating behavior is often repetitive and unconscious. We must be careful what we set our mind on for that is what we will become. Thought patterns must be changed before one's actions are altered. All change first takes place in one's mind. Repentance that turns one from a life of sin to God begins with the mind.

Sow a thought—reap an act

Sow an act—reap a character

Sow a character—reap a destiny

Behavior cannot be separated from one's thoughts. "For as a man thinks in his heart so is he..." (Prov 23:7). Emotions are triggered by thoughts. You can change your mood by changing your thoughts. Right thinking is essential to emotional health and spiritual wellbeing.

3. SPEECH

> "A lying tongue" (6:17), "A false witness who speaks lies…" (6:19).

The scripture declares, "A righteous man hates lying" (Prov 13:5). There is nothing that will destroy relationships any quicker than a lying tongue and a false witness. The "new man" in Christ is admonished to this standard: "Putting away lying, let each one speak truth with his neighbor, for we are members one of another" (Eph 4:25).

> "A false witness will not go unpunished, and he who speaks lies will not escape" (Prov 19:5).

"Many a blunt word has a sharp edge. Keep your words soft and sweet; you never know when you may have to eat them." **(Source Unknown)**

4. RELATIONSHIPS.

> "Hands that shed innocent blood" (6:17). "Feet that are swift in running to evil" (6:18).

These verses describe one who shows no regard for the interest, wellbeing, or feelings of others. "Self-interest is the enemy of all true affections." (Tacitus)

"To be trusted is a greater compliment than to be loved." **(George McDonald)**

> "Let each of you look out not only for his own interest, but also for the interest of others" (Phil 2:4).

1 Corinthians 13 speaks of love: "Love…does not behave rudely,

does not seek its own, is not provoked, thinks no evil" (1 Cor 13:4). Love liberates; once loved, a believer is liberated from the bondage to self-interest to love and serve others.

5. ORGANIZATIONALLY.

"One who sows discord among brethren" (6:19).

"Go from the presence of a foolish man, when you do not perceive in him the lips of knowledge" (Prov 14:7). It is difficult for discord to be sown if one's ear is unavailable.

"Divisiveness breeds weakness." **(Donald Phillips,** *Lincoln on Leadership***)**

"When love prevails among believers, especially in times of strong disagreement, it presents to the world an indisputable mark of a true follower of Jesus Christ." (*Our Daily Bread, Oct. 4, 1992*)

Changing Self-Defeating Behavior

Hate what God hates (Prov 6:16; Ps 97:10; Prov 8:13)

Love what God loves (Heb 1:8–9)

Exalt God's word above all else (Ps 1)

15

Preparing for Increase
Isaiah 54:1–17

In verses 1–6 God's people are addressed as a woman whose period of barrenness is over. The desolation and reproach of her widowhood has ended. She is instructed to prepare for increase. The time to favor her has come.

> "For you shall expand to the right and to the left...the desolate cities will be inhabited" (54:3).

There are four preparations to be made in advance of the promised increase. Failure to prepare for increase sets one up not to experience the increase that is promised.

1. SPREAD OUT.

> "Enlarge the place of your tent" (54:2).

Allow the promise of God to raise your level of expectation. Take action in response to God's promise of increase. Don't think less; think more—make room in your thinking for increase—see beyond your current limitations. Don't allow your past to dictate the size of your future. Enlarge your dream until it honors God and horrifies you.

Take a step of faith in response to the promise. "Enlarge the place of your tent": prepare for the increase that has been promised. Don't wait and see—take action that prepares to see—believe that what God has promised he is able to perform (Rom 4:21).

2. STRETCH OUT.

"Let them stretch out the curtains of your dwelling" (54:2).

Allow your mind to be enlarged with God-sized possibilities. Dream beyond the boundaries of your current barrenness. Don't allow fear to keep you from what God has promised. Go ahead, take a step of faith—increase your dwelling to receive God-sized dreams.

> "Do not fear, for you will not be ashamed; neither be disgraced, for you will not be put to shame; for you will forget the shame of your youth, and will not remember the reproach of your widowhood anymore" (54:4).

"Minds are like rubber bands, only useful when stretched." **(Source Unknown)**

"A man's mind stretched to a new idea never goes back to its original dimensions." **(Oliver Wendell Holmes)**

Every achievement of mankind began as a thought in someone's mind. God stretches our minds with his promises.

3. SELL OUT.

"Do not spare" (54:3).

Don't hesitate, don't hold back, go for it! Make a commitment to pursue the dream of increase that God has promised. Your commitment to pursue will never exceed God's ability to provide. Honor God by not holding back or hesitating. Take God at His word, this pleases Him. Complacency is the result of failure to commit.

"Complacency is a blight that zaps energy, dulls attitudes, and causes a drain on the brain. The first symptom is satisfaction with things as they are. The second is rejection of things as they might be. 'Good enough' becomes today's watchword and tomorrow's standard. Complacency makes people fear the unknown, mistrust the untried, and abhor the new. Like water, complacent people follow the easiest course...downhill. They draw false strength from looking back." (*Bits & Pieces*, **May 28, 1992, p. 15**)

"There is one degree between hot water and boiling water. Commitment will get you the extra degree." **(Author Unknown)**

4. STAKE OUT.

"Lengthen your cords and strengthen your stakes" (54:2).

The structure portrayed is a metaphor for the church. Christ is the center pole and the key to the structure (Zech 10:4). The center pole or "tent peg," according to Zechariah, refers to the large stake within the center of a tent that provides the necessary brace to hold up the tent.

The cords to be lengthened are attached to the center pole and represent various ministries within the church. The ministries are secured to stakes. The stakes are people to whom the ministries are assigned. It is imperative that these "stakes" (i.e., people) are firmly secured in the soil of the local church. The success of the church's ministry is directly in proportion to the staying power of these stakes. The stakes must be strengthened, strong and steady. If the stakes are moved the entire structure is placed in jeopardy.

These stakes must be secured deep in the soil of Christ and His church.

The increase has been promised. Preparation to receive the increase must be made in advance. You must "do" before you "see."

"Preparedness is the key to success and victory." **(Douglas MacArthur)**

16

Unlock Your Future
Isaiah 51:1–23

The people of God sometimes find themselves living in a place of less than God's best for them. Isaiah 51 announces the release of God's people into a future that God has designed for them.

> "So the ransomed of the Lord shall return and come to Zion with singing, with everlasting joy on their heads, they shall obtain joy and gladness; sorrow and sighing shall flee away" (51:11).

The prophet Isaiah reveals four keys that will unlock the future that God has designed for His people.

1. LISTEN UP.

> "Listen to Me, you who follow after righteousness, you who seek the Lord…" (51:1).

> "Listen to Me, My people; and give ear to Me, o My

nation..." (51:4).

"Listen to Me, you who know righteousness, You people in whose heart is My law; Do not fear the reproach of men, nor be afraid of their insults" (51:7).

Whoever has your ear holds your future. When we listen to God, we hear opportunity and receive instruction. Three times we are admonished to "listen." When we listen, faith comes and fear is lessened. (51:7–8, 12–16). When we hear God's voice, we can do His will, because we know His will.

2. LOOK UP.

"Look to Abraham your father, and to Sarah who bore you; for I called him alone, and blessed him and increased him" (51:2).

"Lift up your eyes to the heavens..." (51:6).

Look to your heritage, Abraham (51:1,2) what I have done for him, I will do for you. Follow his example. Believe what I have promised. (Rom 4:17–21).

Look up to the heavens, gain God's perspective (51:6). Whatever has your focus has your faith and your future. The longer you look at God, the smaller your problem gets.

"Looking unto Jesus, the author and finisher of our faith..." (Heb 12:2).

"Set your mind on things above, not on things on the earth" (Col 3:2).

3. WAKE UP.

"Awake, awake, put on strength, O arm of the Lord, Awake as in the ancient days, in the generations of old. Are you

> not the arm that cut Rahab apart, and wounded the serpent?" (51:9).

> "Awake, awake! Stand up. O Jerusalem, you who have drunk at the hand of the Lord the cup of his fury..." (51:17).

Verse 9 instructs us to call on God to awaken and to demonstrate the strength of His arm in securing the release of His people. Verse 17 calls for God's people to wake up to their condition and circumstances and to what God is about to accomplish for them.

God is alerting His people to a shift that is about to occur in their lives. Things are about to change for the better. God alerts His people to awake to His favor and time of their blessing.

> "A little sleep, a little slumber, a little folding of the hands to sleep—so shall poverty come on you like a prowler, and your need like an armed man" (Prov 6:10–11).

To be asleep is to be unaware of what is happening around you. God calls for His people to awaken to the possibilities that He is presenting to them. He is unlocking their future—releasing His best. We must be awake and alert or we will miss God's good promises and our destiny.

4. STAND UP.

> "Awake, awake! Stand up, O Jerusalem..." (51:17).

It is time to stand up rather than to lie down, allowing the enemy to walk over you like dirt in the street.

> "See, I have taken out of your hand the cup of trembling, the dregs of the cup of my fury; you shall no longer drink it. But I will put it in the hand of those who afflict you, who have said to you, 'lie down, that we may walk over you.'

And you have laid your body like the ground, and as the street for those who walk over you" (51:22–23).

Things are changing. The cup of God's wrath is being passed to your oppressor, and the time of favor and restoration has come. Stand up. It's time for you to be the head and not the tail. It is time for you to be above and not beneath (Deut 28:13). The enemy is to be under our feet.

> "Behold I give you the authority to trample on serpents and scorpions, and over all the power of the enemy, and nothing shall by any means hurt you" (Luke 10:19).

Stand up! Stand in your place as the people of God. Don't let the devil trample on you like dirt in the street. Stand up—walk in the authority Christ has given. Quit the victim role—stand up in the victorious role.

17

Maintaining Your Spiritual Edge
Ecclesiastes 10:10

"If the ax is dull, and one does not sharpen the edge, then he must use more strength; but wisdom brings success" (Eccl 10:10).

Wisdom sharpens an ax when it is dull. Without wisdom you must work harder. An ax becomes dull through use, abuse, or lack of use. In any case, a dull ax must be sharpened.

Like an ax, Christians must maintain their spiritual edge. God sharpened the "ax" of his church on the day of Pentecost. When the spiritual edge (the Pentecostal experience) is lost, more effort is required.

Christians must learn to associate with those who will sharpen rather than dull their edge. "As iron sharpens iron, so a man sharpens the countenance of his friend" (Prov 27:17). The opposite is also true. The wrong friends will dull your spiritual edge.

The enemies of God want to keep God's people from having weapons that are sharp and effective (1 Sam 13:19–23). There are three reasons for an ax in scripture—the battle ax (Jer 51:20), the breaker ax (used to destroy idolatrous images) (2 Chron 34:1–7), and the building ax (2 Kings 6:1–7).

Regaining Lost Power
2 Kings 6:1–7

1. ACKNOWLEDGE THE LOSS. (6:5)

> "But as one was cutting down a tree, the iron ax head fell into the water; and he cried out and said, Alas, master! For it was borrowed."

God's power is always loaned, never owned. The worker was painfully aware that he had lost the ax head. The work could not continue until the ax head was recovered.

The first step to recovering lost power is to acknowledge that it has been lost. The church at Ephesus was instructed by the Lord how to recover lost love. (See Rev 2:1–7). Lost power is recovered in the same manner.

2. CRY FOR HELP. (6:5)

> "And he cried out and said, alas, master! For it was borrowed" (6:5*)*.

As soon as the worker was aware of the loss, he asked for help. Jesus promised he would give the Holy Spirit to those who ask (Lk 11:13). When the Holy Spirit is consistently asked for, he is consistently given. This ensures that you keep the spiritual edge. The Lord has compassion on those who lose their power.

> "For the Lord will judge His people and have compassion on His servants, when He sees that their power is gone…"

(Deut 32:36).

One New Year's Day, in the Tournament of Roses parade, a beautiful float suddenly sputtered and quit. It was out of gas. The whole parade was held up until someone could get a can of gas. The amusing thing was that this float represented the Standard Oil Company. With all its vast oil resources, its truck was out of gas.

Christians often neglect their spiritual maintenance, and though they are "clothed with power" (Lk 24:49), they find themselves out of gas. (**Steve Blankenship** states in *God Came Near* **by Max Lucado**, Multnomah Press, 1987, p. 95.)

3. RETURN TO WHERE YOU LOST IT. (6:6)

> "So the man of God said, "Where did it fall? And he showed him the place..." (6:6).

When we lose something, we retrace our steps in hopes of finding it. Elijah begins the recovery by having the worker point out the exact place he lost the ax head. Jacob had his spiritual edge restored when he returned to Bethel (Gen 35:1–5). The prodigal son was restored when he returned to the father. "The place" where we lost our power may not be a geographical place, but a place of the heart. A place where we lost the spiritual edge.

4. EXPECT A POSITIVE RESPONSE. (6:6b)

A supernatural response. "So he (Elisha) cut off a stick, and threw it in there, and he made the iron to float" (KJV, "to swim") (6:6b). The prophetic act brought the ax head to the surface and placed it within reach of recovery.

Jesus said to the woman at the well, who had described the water as out of His reach, "having nothing to draw with, and the well is deep" (Jn 4:11), "If you knew the gift of God, and who it is who says to you, Give me a drink; you would have asked Him, and He would have given you living water" (Jn 4:10).

5. REACH OUT AND TAKE IT FOR YOURSELF. (6:7)

"Therefore he said, pick it up for yourself. So he reached out his hand and took it" (6:7).

Faith reaches for what is offered and takes it. The ax head had been placed within the worker's reach—now the worker must reach out and take it to himself. Now the work can continue.

Jesus instructed the church to wait in Jerusalem until they were clothed with power from on high, and then they could continue his great work. When one works and serves without the ax being sharpened, one must use the energy of the flesh.

"In a seminary mission's class, Herbert Jackson told how, as a new missionary, he was assigned a car that would not start without a push. After pondering his problem, he devised a plan. He went to the school near his home, got permission to take some children out of class, and had them push his car off. As he made his rounds, he would either park on a hill or leave the engine running. He used this ingenious procedure for two years.

"Ill health forced the Jackson family to leave, and a new missionary came to that station. When Jackson proudly began to explain his arrangement for getting the car started, the new man began looking under the hood. Before the explanation was complete, the new missionary interrupted, 'Why, Dr. Jackson, I believe the only trouble is this loose cable.' He gave the cable a twist, stepped into the car, pushed the switch, and to Jackson's astonishment, the engine roared to life. For two years needless trouble had become routine. The power was there all the time. Only a loose connection kept Jackson from putting that power to work."

J. B. Phillips paraphrases Ephesians 1:19–20, 'How tremendous is the power available to us who believe in God.' When we make firm our connection with God, his life and power flow through us."
(**Earnest B. Beevers,** *SermonIllustrations.com*)

18

How to Break a Drought
1 Kings 18:17–46

Elijah announced a drought in chapter 17. "There shall not be neither dew nor rain these years, except at my word" (17:1).

Israel's sin is the cause for the drought. There are similarities between natural droughts and spiritual droughts that Christians face. There are seven steps to breaking a drought.

1. TAKE RESPONSIBILITY. (18:17)

> "Then it happened, when Ahab saw Elijah, that Ahab said to him, Is that you, o troubler of Israel?" (18:17).

Taking personal responsibility for one's spiritual condition is the first step to improvement. Ahab refused to take responsibility for his role in causing Israel's drought, spiritually and literally. The nation was hurting, and Ahab refused all responsibility.

2. RESTORE OBEDIENCE. (18:18)

> "I have not troubled Israel, but you and your father's house
> have, in that you have forsaken the commandments of the
> lord and have followed Baals" (18:18).

Obedience brings the blessing of God, while disobedience dries it
up. According to Deuteronomy 28 the blessings of God are
conditioned. Obedience is essential to having the blessing of God.

> "And all these blessings shall come upon you and overtake
> you, Because you obey the voice of the Lord your God"
> (Deut 28:2).

> "The Lord will open to you His good treasure, the heavens,
> to give the rain to your land in its season—If you heed the
> commandments of the Lord your God, which I command
> you today, and are careful to observe them" (Deut 28:12–
> 13).

In South Africa, naturalist club owner Beau Brummell was irked
by accusations from moral watchdogs that a shriveling Transvaal
drought was brought on by the "sin" of nude togetherness at his
thousand-acre farm. So he asked his 370 visitors to get dressed.
And, for the first time in two months, it poured rain. "It's enough
to make me become a monk!" Brummell said. **(Ingrid Norton in**
Rand Daily Mail, Johannesburg)

3. BE DECISIVE. (18:21)

> "How long will you falter between two opinions? If the
> Lord is God, follow Him, but if Baal, follow him, but the
> people answered not a word" (18:21).

The people's silence revealed their indecisiveness. One's mind must be made up: you can't serve two masters. "A double-minded man is unstable in all his ways" (Jas 1:8,4:8).

"When you have to make a choice and don't make it, that is in itself a choice." **(William James)**

"The words of Eleanor Roosevelt ring true: One's philosophy is not best expressed in words. It is expressed in the choices one makes. In the long run, we shape our lives and we shape ourselves. The process never ends until we die. And the choices we make are ultimately our responsibility." **(Tim Kimmel,** *Little House on the Freeway***)**

4. RETURN TO THE ALTAR. (18:30)

"And he repaired the altar of the Lord that was broken down" (18:30).

The altar of the Lord has fallen into disrepair from neglect, not excessive use. The writer of Hebrews warns us:

"How shall we escape if we neglect so great a salvation, which at first began to be spoken by the Lord and was confirmed to us by those who heard Him" (Heb 2:3).

"Neglect" according to Strong's Concordance means: to be careless, make light of, not regard. Webster: to ignore or disregard, to fail to carry out through carelessness or by intention, to omit, or overlook.

5. MAKE THE SACRIFICE. (18:33)

"And he put the wood in order, cut the bull in pieces, and laid it on the wood" (18:33).

God's people need to "cut the bull" and place it all on the altar of sacrifice. (Pun intended.)

"May not a single moment of my life be spent outside the light, love, and joy of God's presence and not a moment without the entire surrender of myself as a vessel for Him to fill full of His Spirit and His love." **(Andrew Murray)**

6. REMOVE THE IDOLS. (18:37)

"You have turned their hearts back to you again" (18:37).

An idol is anything that cools our passion for Christ. Idols are destroyed when the Lord is returned to his rightful place in our hearts. Idolatry will cause a drought; remove the idol the drought will end and the rains will come.

7. ENJOY THE RAIN. (18:41)

"Go up, eat and drink: for there is the sound of abundance of rain" (18:41).

The drought is over—the sky is dark—the cold winds are blowing—a heavy rain is falling—the favor and blessings of God have been restored.

"Revival is that sovereignty of God in which He visits His own people, restoring and releasing them into the fullness of His blessing." **(Robert Coleman)**

19

Moving Forward

"And the Lord said to Moses, why do you cry to me? Tell the children of Israel to go forward" (Ex 14:15).

"Playing safe is probably the most unsafe thing in the world, you don't stand still you must go forward." **(Robert Collier)**

The text for this reflection is Exodus chapters 13,14, and15, and Joshua chapter 1. Three things are essential for "moving forward."

1. MOVING FORWARD REQUIRES FAITH.

Circumstances are not often ideal for moving forward. There are obstacles and opposition that seem to defy progress. The Egyptian army is pursuing Israel to return them to slavery, and the Red Sea is blocking their escape. In the midst of all the negatives God speaks, and when God speaks everything changes. The most severe circumstances change for the better when God speaks.

Faith is key to coming into all God has promised. There comes a time when you have labored and prayed enough. The time comes when you simply must rise and move forward.

"Even if you fall on your face, you're still moving forward." **(Victor Kiam)**

Moving Forward in faith involves:

- **Moving from where you are (Ex 14:1–9, 13:3–9)**
"And Moses said to the people: Remember this day in which you went out of Egypt, out of the house of bondage; for by strength of hand the Lord brought you out of this place..." (Ex 13:3).

- **Moving beyond the obstacles (Ex 14:8, 10–31)**
"And Moses said to the people: Do not be afraid, stand still, and see the salvation of the Lord, which He will accomplish for you today.

 For the Egyptians whom you see today, you will never see again no more forever" (Ex 14:13).

- **Moving forward according to promise. (Ex 14:31, 15:17)**
"You will bring them in and plant them in the mountain of your inheritance, in the place, Lord, which You have made for Your own dwelling, the sanctuary, O Lord, which your hands have established" (Ex 15:17).

2. MOVING FORWARD REQUIRES FORMATION.

"So God led the people around by way of the wilderness of the Red Sea, and the children of Israel went up in orderly ranks out of the land of Egypt" (Ex 13:18).

You don't move millions of people through desert terrain without some sort of structure and organization.

"Let all things be done decently and in order" (1 Cor 14:40). Three truths appear in this nine-word sentence. 1) Let all things be done, let nothing be left undone that should be done. 2) Let all things be done decently. 3) Let all things be done decently and in order. The word "order" implies dignity, which is achieved by fixed and orderly succession. It means to be arranged in an orderly manner. The word implies quality, style, excellence. The right thing, the right time, the right way.

3. MOVING FORWARD REQUIRES FAITHFULNESS.

"So they answered Joshua, saying, all that you command us we will do, and wherever you send us we will go" (Josh 1:16).

Fast forwarding, Joshua and the children of Israel are encamped at the Jordan River. The river is at its annual flood stage, and God miraculously parts the waters once again to allow Israel to cross.

The leaders of Israel come to Joshua and assure him of their commitment to faithfulness and support of his leadership. Faithfulness is the key to achievement. Leadership at every level must serve as an example of faithfulness. Faithful in the small, insignificant things. Faithful in the unseen or hidden things. Faithful in what is another man's. Faithful in all matters dealing with money.

No matter how pleasant or difficult it is where you are currently—you must move on. You must move from the familiar to the frightening, from the comfortable to the challenging if you are going to gain new territory for God. The message of God to his people in every generation is "keep moving forward."

"We keep moving forward, opening new doors, and doing new things, because we're curious and curiosity keeps leading us down new paths." **(Walt Disney)**

20

A Winning Team

There is little difference between winning teams and losing teams. Among professional bowlers there is only a 5 percent difference between those bowlers who go home and those who bowl in the finals. Only 5 percent is a small difference to separate winners from losers.

There are four essential components to being a winning team.

1. THE HEAD OF A WINNING TEAM.

Games are won or lost between the ears before any player reaches the field. A team's performance can rise no higher than the level of its thinking. The mindset of a team sets the ceiling of the team's achievements. Thoughts are either limiting or liberating, empowering or paralyzing. A team must think like winners to be winners.

"The deciding voice in determining your success is not your supporters or your opponents. It's the internal voice that limits or lifts you." **(Howard Bass,** Tampa, Florida**)**

What You Think of Yourself Is Important!

Dr. Archibald D. Hart, in his book *Habits of the Mind,* has this to say about the influence of our thoughts: "let me put the issue to you in a nutshell: who you are, as a Christian believer, can be no better and no worse than the thoughts you entertain in your head. Who you are emotionally can never transcend your level of thinking. Your thought process is a ceiling beyond which you cannot aspire. Your brain is no stronger than your weakest thought, and your character no more victorious than your most private reflection."

"All that a man achieves and all that a man fails to achieve is the direct result of his own thoughts. You are today where your thoughts have brought you. You will be tomorrow where your thoughts take you." **(James Allen)**

A winning team has its head in the right place—on winning and nothing less. Winning teams play to win—winning teams think winning.

2. THE HEART OF A WINNING TEAM.

Every great achievement is fueled by passion. Passion changes losers into winners. Passion makes possible the impossible. Passion is the energy of the soul, the fire in one's belly.

"Intensity coupled with commitment is magnetic." **(Warren Bennis)**

"The greatest crippler of inspiring others is lack of passion." **(Source Unknown)**

> "And whatever you do, do it heartily, as to the Lord and not to men, knowing that from the Lord you will receive the reward of the inheritance; for you serve the Lord Christ" (Col. 3:23–24).

"One person with passion is better than forty people merely interested." (**E.M. Forster,** English novelist)

"Purpose may point you in the right direction, but it's passion that propels you." (**Travis McAshan,** entrepreneur)

3. THE HABITS OF A WINNING TEAM.

Winning habits make for winning teams. Poor habits produce poor teams. Average habits, an average team. Exceptional habits, an exceptional team. Habits define teams. Habits are formed by repetition. Habits are what we do without thinking.

Help With Your Habits

"A large portion of your life is automatically run by your habits. It has been estimated by experts that 80 percent of everything we do from the time we get up until we go to bed is out of habit. A habit helps us to repeat the behavior automatically without having to think or to learn all over again. A habit is a thought or action that we have repeated until it has become automatic, and we do it without stopping to decide.

Habits can:

- Be your friend or be your enemy
- Help you or hurt you
- Serve you or enslave you
- Work for you or work against you
- Aid you in your Christian witness or damage your Christian witness"

(Dare to Discipline Yourself, by **Dale E. Galloway**, published by Revell)

"Bad habits are like comfortable beds...easy to get into but hard to get out of." (**Source Unknown**)

4. THE HANDS OF A WINNING TEAM.

There comes a time for every team to take the field ball in hand. Theory, practice, planning, and preparation must culminate in action. King David instructed his son Solomon, "Be strong and do it." (1 Chron 28:10). The plans for the temple had been drawn, the material gathered, and the workers assembled. Now it was time for Solomon to *"Be strong and do it."* Take the plow in your hand and go for it. (Luke 9:62, 1 Cor 9:10). The hands of a winning team are not idle (Prov 20:4, 6:10, 12:14, 21:25-26). The promise of God is, "He will bless the work of your hands" (Deut 28:12).

There are three kinds of workers, for example, when a piano is to be moved: the first kind gets behind and pushes, the second pulls and guides, the third grabs the piano stool. **(Source Unknown)**

"You don't want to be like this. A sign in the window read: **No Help Wanted**. As two men passed by, one said to the other, 'you should apply, you would be great.'" (*Decision Making & The Will of God*)

Winning teams work hard at winning. Losing doesn't require nearly the effort and determination as winning.

"When you live for a strong purpose, the hard work isn't an option, it's a necessity." **(Source Unknown)**

21

The Ministry of Maturity
Hebrews 6:1-3

"Let us go on to perfection" (i.e., maturity).

Maturity in a biological sense means to become full grown. Maturity indicates that the person, plant, or animal has reached the full potential inherent in its species or nature. Christian maturity is when the believer reaches the full potential inherent in the new nature.

The mandate of ministry is the maturity of the saints (Eph 4:11–13). The focus of preaching is the maturity of the saints (Col 1:28). The passion of pastoral prayer is the maturity of the saints (Col 4:12). The philosophy of ministry is shaped by the maturity of the saints (Eph 4:7-16).

1. THE COMMAND.

"Therefore, let us go on to perfection."

This exhortation is in the imperative mode, therefore, a

command—a strong exhortation for the church to pursue maturity. The exhortation is also a choice to be made. The exhortation is inclusive. Let us all, the entire congregation, go on to maturity.

The Five Marks of Immaturity

The "therefore" refers the reader back to chapter 5 of Hebrews, which lists five marks of the immature. These five marks of immaturity must be put away if one is to pursue maturity as a Christian. The five marks of immaturity are:

- Dull of hearing (5:11)
- Inability to instruct others (5:12)
- Constant diet of milk (5:12–13)
- Unable to apply Biblical truth (5:14)
- Perpetually dependent on others (5:14)

2. THE CHALLENGE.

In his book, *The Leader Within*, **Pat Riley**, famed coach of the NBA, gave some innovations to improve his team's performance during the 1986–87 season. He selected five areas of performance that had cost his team the championship the previous year. He then challenged each player to put in enough effort to gain one percentage point in each of the five areas. He told the players, "Don't try to go 10 percent above and don't let yourself go 10 percent below it. Just concentrate on a moderate, sustainable improvement." A one percent improvement in five areas, for twelve players, could give them 60 percent increased performance over the previous year!

Five Marks of Maturity

Maturity can be achieved by moderate, sustainable improvement in five areas.

- Scripture reading
- Prayer
- Serving (witnessing)
- Fasting
- Giving (tithing)

It is a worthy goal for all believers to regularly participate in these five Christian disciplines in order to achieve and sustain the process of maturity.

3. THE COMMITMENT.

The commitment to maturity is a commitment to be a lifelong student of scripture. According to 2 Timothy 3:16–17, there are five benefits derived from the study of scripture.

Five Benefits of Scripture

- Accurate and reliable truth to direct one's belief and behavior (doctrine)
- Reprimand of wrong belief and behavior (reproof)
- Clarity for correcting wrong beliefs and behavior (correction)
- Real facts to support proper belief and behavior (instruction)
- Thoroughly supplying what is required for every good work (equipping)

When the word of God is received, planted, and applied consistently to one's life, the result is progress toward maturity.

22

Multiplication Follows Consecration
John 6:1–14

The feeding of the five thousand with five loaves and two small fish is a miracle of multiplication. However, before there was multiplication there was consecration of the five loaves and two fish.

1. CHRIST TAKES WHAT IS OFFERED TO HIM. (6:11)

"And Jesus took the loaves..."

The loaves and fish were freely and willingly offered to Jesus. There was a transfer of ownership. They had belonged to the young man who brought them, now they belong to Jesus. Like the loaves and fish, a life freely and willingly given to Jesus becomes a life consecrated to him.

Prayer of Consecration

"May not a single moment of my life be spent outside the light, love, and joy of God's presence and not a moment without entire surrender of myself as a vessel for Him to fill full of His spirit and love." **(Andrew Murray)**

2. CHRIST BREAKS WHAT HE TAKES.

Three of the four gospels have Jesus clearly portrayed as "breaking" the loaves and fish. Breaking is also implied in John's gospel (Mt 14:19; Mk 6:41; Lk 9:16).

Christ transforms what he receives. Nothing remains as it was previously. A life given to Jesus changes for the better. Christ rearranges, redefines, and redirects the life consecrated to him.

> "For whoever desires to save his life will lose it, but whoever loses his life for my sake will find it" (Mt 16:25).

3. CHRIST BLESSES WHAT HE TAKES.

"He took the five loaves and two fish, and looking up to Heaven, he blessed and broke and gave the loaves to the disciples, and the disciples gave to the multitudes" (Mt 14:19).

Once consecrated, the loaves and fish are blessed. The consecrated life is a blessed life—one that blesses others. A life ready and willing to be distributed to others. The blessing that follows consecration should be the desire of all who serve the savior, Jesus Christ (1 Chron 4:9–10). God blesses the life that belongs to him (Gen 22:17–18).

"I have held many things in my hand, and have lost them all; but whatever I have placed in God's hand that I still possess." **(Martin Luther)**

4. CHRIST SATIFIES WITH WHAT HE MULTIPLIES. (6:11–12)

> "And Jesus took the loaves, and when He had given thanks He distributed them to the disciples, and the disciples to those sitting down; and likewise of the fish, as much as they wanted. So when they were filled, He said to His disciples, 'Gather up the fragments that remain, so that nothing is lost.'"

The multitudes were filled with as much fish and bread as they wanted. The hungry and weary are refreshed with that which is placed in Christ's hands. That which belongs to Jesus feeds and satisfies others (Jn 21:15–18).

5. CHRIST PRESERVES WHAT IS HIS. (6:12–13)

> "Therefore they gathered them up, and filled twelve baskets with the fragments of the five barley loaves which were left over by those who had eaten" (6:13).

Nothing is lost and nothing wasted. What remained will satisfy another day. Christ preserves the life consecrated to him.

> "You did not choose Me, but I chose you and appointed you that you should go and bear fruit, and that your fruit should remain…"(Jn 15:16).

As Christ received glory for feeding the multitudes, He receives glory for every life consecrated to Him.

"It doesn't take great men to do great things; it only takes consecrated men." **(Philipps Brooks)**

23

Wise Council
1 Corinthians 14:40

"Let all things be done decently and in order" (14:40*).*

In the nine words of our text there are three nuggets of wise counsel for all who would lead God's church.

1. LET ALL THINGS BE "DONE."

There are things that need to be done in a vital and vibrate ministry. Paul's counsel—let them be done. Let nothing go undone that needs to be done. The little things, the unseen things, the mundane things, all things. Let them all be done.

Slothfulness will destroy a church, a home, or a business. Heavy equipment is not required to demolish a church. Neglect will have the same outcome. Neglect will take longer, but the outcome is the same (Prov 18:9, 24:30–34). Paul's counsel is—"He who leads, do so with diligence" (Rom 12:8).

"Not lagging in diligence, fervent in spirit, serving the

Lord" (Rom 12:11).

"Diligence" is defined as careful attention to detail—a persevering effort. This type of effort will preserve the church from the neglect of slothfulness.

2. LET ALL THINGS BE DONE "DECENTLY."

"Decently" is an adverb. A verb describes action, and an adverb describes how the action is performed. "Decently" describes that action which is proper, fitting, well done, suitable, according to acceptable standards.

The way we do things can be as significant as what we are doing. Dignity and decorum are always in order.

To be fervent in spirit is to be "fired up" in one's service for Christ. The word means to boil with heat. It is a metaphor for being boiling hot with love and zeal. Service for Christ is to be conducted with passion.

> "And whatever you do, do it heartily, as to the Lord and not to men" (Col 3:23).

Serving the Lord is the motive for one's passion and attention to details. Christ has given His best, and we in turn give Him our best.

"The difference between something good and something great is attention to detail." (**Charles Swindol)**

3. LET ALL THINGS BE DONE DECENTLY AND "IN ORDER."

> "For this reason I left you in Crete, that you should set in order the things that are lacking..." (Titus 1:5).

"For though I am absent in the flesh, yet I am with you in spirit, rejoicing to see your good order and the steadfastness of your faith in Christ" (Col 2:5).

Order can be referred to as an official dignity. It means to put persons and things into their proper place in relationship to each other. To place in order is to arrange the whole so that it works as a unit with each element having a proper function.

When Israel left Egypt they "went up in orderly ranks out of the land of Egypt" (Ex 13:18). You don't move millions of people through the desert without some form of order, structure, organization, and precepts to follow. This is true of the church of the living God (1Tim 3:15). Order is essential to the success of any organization.

"In order" is a state or condition in which everything is in its rightful place and functioning properly. It is the opposite of disorder. It means to arrange in an orderly manner so that what is done is done in the right way at the right time. Order speaks of quality, style, and excellence.

"Spirituality" is more often associated with spontaneity than with order and structure. However, order and structure preserve the authentic move of the spirit (1 Cor 14:40).

"For God is not the author of confusion (disorder), but of peace, as in all the churches of the saints" (1 Cor 14:33).

A final word concerning "spirit and structure": 1) structure without the spirit is death, 2) the spirit without structure is disaster, and 3) the spirit with structure is dynamite.

24

Be Strong and Do It
1 Chronicles 28:1–21

"Consider now, for the Lord has chosen you to build a house for the sanctuary; be strong, and do it" (28:10).

The final two chapters of First Chronicles, chapters 28 and 29, contain David's instruction to his son Solomon concerning the building of God's house. David's instruction contains: promise, priorities, and provision.

1. THE PROMISE.

"Now he said to me, 'it is your son Solomon who shall build My house and My courts; for I have chosen him to be My son, and I will be his father. Moreover I will establish his kingdom forever, if he is steadfast to observe My commandments and My judgments, as it is this day'" (28:6–7).

The promise is "Your son Solomon shall build My house" (28:6). As Solomon fulfills the condition of being "steadfast to observe My commandments and My judgments," God will fulfill the promise. As we obey God's precepts we possess his promise.

"You can't break God's promises by leaning on them." (**Source Unknown**)

2. THE PRIORITIES.

> "As for you, my son Solomon, know the God of your father, and serve Him with a loyal heart and with a willing mind: for the Lord searches all hearts and understands all the intent of the thoughts. If you seek Him, He will be found by you; but if you forsake Him, He will cast you off forever. Consider now, for the Lord has chosen you to build a house for the sanctuary; be strong and do it" (28:9–10).

David sets forth five priorities that will assure Solomon's success if he embraces and follows through with them.

- Know God
- Serve Him
- Seek Him
- Be strong
- Do it

> "And David said to his son Solomon, be strong and of good courage, and do it, do not fear or be dismayed, for the Lord God—my God—will be with you. He will not leave you nor forsake you, until you have finished all the work for the service of the house of the Lord" (28:20).

Courage is doing what you should even when you're afraid to do it. God honors courage. Courage is contagious—when champions stand, others will follow.

Four Qualities of the Courageous
(Ray Pritchard)

- Bravery in the face of danger: "I won't be afraid"
- Steadfastness in the face of opposition: "I won't give up"
- Action in the face of resistance: "I won't be intimated"
- Optimism in the face of despair: "I won't lose heart"

3. THE PROVISION.

Solomon is assured of everything essential to completing his assignment to build God's house. There are eight essential provisions given to ensure the project is a success.

- The Lord's presence (28:20)
- The plans for construction (28:11–19)
- Craftsmen to do the work (28:21)
- Leaders to lead the workers (28:21)
- People essential to the work (28:21)
- Money to pay for the construction (28:14–18; 29:19)
- The anointing that enables (28:21–25)

In light of all that has been promised there is only one thing that remains: "Be strong and do it!"

Dr. J.B. Gambrel tells an amusing story from General Stonewall Jackson's famous valley campaign. Jackson's army found itself on one side of a river when it needed to be on the other side. After telling his engineers to plan and build a bridge so the army could cross, he called his wagon master in to tell him that it was urgent the wagon train cross the river as soon as possible. The wagon master started gathering all the logs, rocks, and fence rails he could find and built a bridge. Long before daylight General Jackson was told by his wagon master that all the wagons and artillery had crossed the river. General Jackson asked, where are the engineers and what are they doing? The wagon master's only reply was that they were in their tent drawing up plans for a bridge.

25

The Man of God
1 Kings 13:1–32

The term "man of God" appears fifteen times in the text. The unnamed man of God serves to illustrate the high cost of disobedience. The unnamed man of God represents the possibility of all men of God.

"The cost of obedience is nothing compared with the cost of disobedience." **(Richard Baxter)**

1. THE MAN OF GOD AND THE KING. (13:1–10)

As King Jeroboam is about to offer a sacrifice to a pagan deity, the unnamed man of God speaks the message of God and "crie[s] out against the altar." When Jeroboam stretches out his arm to point out the man and have him arrested, his arm is paralyzed in midair. Jeroboam requests that the man of God "entreat the favor of the Lord, that my hand may be restored" (13:6).

Jeroboam's arm is restored and the man of God is invited to the palace for rest, food, and a gift from the king. In obedience to the instruction he received from God prior to coming, the man of God declines the offer and leaves.

As we shall see later in the narrative, a single previous act of obedience does not guarantee future obedience.

"The first duty of every soul is to find not its freedom, but its master." **(Peter T. Forsythe)**

2. THE MAN OF GOD AND THE OLD PROPHET. (13:11–22)

When the sons of the old prophet tell the story of the man of God and the king, the old prophet saddles his donkey and pursues the man of God. The old prophet finds the man of God sitting under an oak tree.

The man of God accepts uncritically the older prophet's word, failing to test spirits (1 Jn 4:1). The sad result is the death of the disobedient prophet (13:23–25) and the shame and disgrace of the older prophet (13:29–32).

We can learn several lessons from the experience of the man of God and the old prophet.

- Delayed obedience is disobedience.
  The old prophet delays the hasty exit of the man of God as instructed by the Lord (15–19).

- Partial obedience is disobedience.
  The man of God refuses the king's invitation, but not the invitation of the old prophet. The old prophet deceives the man of God with lies (v18).

- Misguided obedience is disobedience.
  The old prophet deceives the man of God by concealing his lies with scriptural or spiritual overtones. Failing to stand on the word he had received, the man of God falls into disobedience.

It is hard to argue with someone when they play "the God card." People are deceived into disobedience when God or the Bible is used to justify actions and behavior. Discernment is essential to obedience (Lk 4:9–12). People who play "the God card" will not usually listen to counsel until their disobedience results in tragedy.

3. THE MAN OF GOD, THE LION, AND THE DONKEY. (13:23–32)

As the "man of God" travels home, he is met by a lion that kills him. His corpse is left in the road. The lion and the donkey he rode stand there in suspended animation. Those who pass by view the strange scene and pass the story on to others.

The scene was frozen to ensure that all who saw it, heard of it, or read of it would have the tragic scene etched in their memory. The message of the scene is clear. Disobedience has tragic consequences.

Whether a king, a prophet, or a man of God, obedience leads to blessings—disobedience to tragedy.

"It is a great deal easier to do that which God gives us to do, no matter how hard it is, than to face the responsibility of not doing it." (**Dr. B.J. Miller,** *Today in the World*)

26

The Generosity of God
Matthew 7:7–12

Generosity is defined as a willingness or a predisposition to give. It is to be big- hearted, magnanimous, lavish, unsparing, open-hearted, and open-handed (Ps 104:24–28).

1. THE HUMAN BEING IS CAPABLE OF TREMENDOUS ACTS OF GENEROSITY. (7:11)

"If you then, being evil, know how to give good gifts..." (7:11)

Two strangers met on a pier, a friendship developed, and it turned out that one of the new friends needed a kidney transplant. The new friend happened to match and gave his kidney to his new friend.

A young boy was asked if he would give his blood for his sister's transfusion that she might live. During the procedure the sister responded immediately. When the boy saw his sister's progress, he asked, "Will I die now?" He didn't know that his blood was circulating back into his body.

2. THE HEAVENLY FATHER HAS AN EVEN GREATER CAPACITY FOR GENEROSITY. (7:11)

"How much more will your Father who is in heaven give good things to them that ask Him" (7:11).

- The contrast between human fathers and the heavenly Father serves as an incentive to faith.
- The contrast also serves as an antidote to fear (Lk 12:32).
- No barriers remain in God's generosity (Rom 8:32).
- The generosity of God encourages us to place our faith in our heavenly Father, not in uncertain riches (1Tim 6:17).

3. BECAUSE OF GOD'S GENEROSITY AND PREDISPOSITION TO GIVE, HIS CHILDREN ARE ENCOURAGED TO ASK FREELY. (7:7–8)

"Ask and it will be given to you, seek and you will find, knock and it will be opened to you. For everyone who asks receives, and he who seeks finds, and to him who knocks it will be opened(Mt.7:78).

Our asking gives occasion to God's willingness to give. Our capacity to ask will not exhaust God's capacity to give (Eph 3:20).

4. THOSE WHO EXPERIENCE GOD'S GENEROSITY SHOULD OVERFLOW IN GENEROSITY TO OTHERS. (7:12)

"Therefore, whatever you want men to do to you, do also to them, for this is the Law and the Prophets" (Mt 7:12).

No one is ever satisfied with only receiving. The purpose of generosity is that it may overflow to others. We experience greater satisfaction when our receiving overflows in giving. Only when we give is our receiving complete (Acts 20:35).

"While you are enriched in everything for all liberality, which causes Thanksgiving through us to God" (2 Cor 9:11).

"Let him who stole steal no longer, but rather let him labor, working with his hands what is good, that he may have something to give him who has need" (Eph 4:28).

"So let each one give as he purposes in his heart, not grudgingly or of necessity; for God loves a cheerful giver" (2 Cor 9:7).

27

The Gift of Sight

Leadership requires the gift of sight. Without the gift of sight, one becomes "a blind leader of the blind." The gift of sight keeps the leader and followers out of the proverbial ditch (Mt 15:14). The gift of "sight" operates in specific areas of leadership.

1. THE GIFT OF "OVERSIGHT."

> "Therefore take heed to yourselves and to all the flock, among which the Holy Spirit has made you overseers, to shepherd the church of God which He purchased with His own blood" (Acts 20:28).

1 Peter 5:2–4; 1 Timothy 3:1–7 and Titus 1:5–9 emphasize the character and roles of those given oversight of God's church. These scriptures place a premium on the character of the overseer.

"Character is much better kept than recovered." (**Thomas Paine**)

2. THE GIFT OF "INSIGHT."

"While we do not look at the things which are seen, but at the things which are not seen, for the things which are seen are temporary, but the things not seen are eternal" (2 Cor 4:18).

When the Holy Spirit assigns "oversight," He gives "insight." Insight is the ability to see and understand clearly the inner working of things, especially through intuitive understanding. Without "insight" the shepherd can't properly care for, protect, guide, and provide for the flock.

"Nothing is more terrible than activity without insight." (**Thomas Carlyle**)

"Discernment—the ability to look beneath the surface to see reality—involves evaluating information or situations, recognizing differences, considering consequences, and thereby making sound judgments. In our humanity, none of us have this kind of wisdom, but the Lord is willing to give us the discernment we need." (**Charles Stanley,** *Discernment Matters*)

3. THE GIFT OF "FORESIGHT."

"A prudent person foresees danger and takes precautions. The simpleton goes blindly on and suffers the consequences" (Prov 22:3 NLT).

"Foresight"—the act of foreseeing. The power to foresee, a looking forward, a thoughtful regard for the future, a prudent forethought.

Foresight is dealing with the future. "Being future oriented is a necessary requirement for leadership—what distinguishes leaders from others is that they not only have an interest in the future, but they have a capacity to deal with the future. This capacity is sometimes called 'foresight'—If we are not continually looking for things in the future, we will never discover them. To seek and keep on seeking remains the basic condition for finding." (Mt 7:7) (**Tom Marshal,** *Understanding Leadership*)

T.E. Lawrence once said, "All men dream, but not equally. Those who dream in the dusty recesses of their minds awake to the day to find it was all vanity. But the dreamers of the day are dangerous men, for they may act out their dreams with open eyes to make it possible." **(Source Unknown)**

28

Take the Lead
Joshua 1:1–18

Joshua served as Moses's assistant, and now it is his time to "take the lead." "The task you faithfully do today gets you ready for what God is preparing for you. (Mt 25:21)" (**Warren Wiersbe,** *With the Word*)

1. THE LEADER'S PLACE. (1:1–2)

"Moses My servant is dead, now therefore, arise..." (1:2).

Joshua is summoned to step into his place of leadership. "Moses My servant is dead." No one leader can bring God's people into all God has for them; it requires a succession of leaders with different gifts and temperaments. "NOW" is the time for Joshua to "take the lead."

2. THE LEADER'S PURPOSE. (1:2–4)

"Arise, go over this Jordan, you and all this people, to the land which I am giving to them—the children of Israel."

The leader's purpose is to bring God's people into everything God has destined for them. A leader will know the place God wants to take His people and he will move in that direction without hesitation or delay. "Now therefore, arise."

3. THE LEADER'S PROMISE. (1:5)

"No man shall be able to stand before you all the days of your life, as I was with Moses, so I will be with you. I will not leave you nor forsake you" (1:5).

God's presence ensures the leader's success. When God is "with" a leader, He will certainly provide the power, protection, and provision needed to complete the assignment. God's promises must be believed and acted upon (Mk 9:23).

4. THE LEADER'S PART. (1:6–9)

To ensure success, the leader is called to "be" something (1:6,7,9).

- **Be Courageous (1:6)**
  Leadership is not for the fearful or faint of heart. The leader's success will be determined by courage, and courage will come from the leader's character and God's promises.

- **Be Consistent (1:7)**
  Obedience to God's word will ensure success. God's commandments are God's enablements—"do not turn from it to the right or to the left, that you may prosper wherever you go."

- **Be Confident (1:9)**
  Knowing God is "with" you gives confidence. The leader's confidence is contagious. When the leader is confident, the

people will catch the confidence themselves. Confidence will create momentum. Momentum will overcome all obstacles and opposition.

5. THE LEADER'S PEOPLE. (1:10–16)

"Then Joshua commanded the officers and the people." The response of the people to Joshua "taking the lead" is given in verses 16–18.

> "Just as we heeded Moses in all things, so we will heed you. Only the Lord your God be with you, as He was with Moses" (1:17).

God's people will buy into God's leaders who will step up and "take the lead."

29

Christ's Final Instructions
Acts 1:1–14

Acts is a sequel to the gospels. All that Jesus began to do and teach is to be continued through His church (Acts 1:1; Jn 14:12).

In His final instructions Christ gives four essential truths that must be established in any congregation aspiring to continue the ministry of Jesus.

1. THE MESSAGE. 1:3

"Speaking to them of the things pertaining to the Kingdom of God" (1:3).

The church is to preach and pursue kingdom realities (Mt 6:33, 10:7; Acts 8:12; Lk 9:2, 10:9). The Kingdom of God destroys the work of Satan and bestows kingdom blessings upon its citizens (Acts 10:38; 1 Jn 3:8). The church is to pray for God's kingdom realities to be established on earth as in Heaven. Where God's kingdom is realized, His name is honored, His will is done, needs are supplied, debts are forgiven, relationships are restored, temptation is overcome, and worship is expressed (Mt 6:9–13).

2. THE MEANS. 1:4–8

"But you shall receive power when the Holy Spirit has come upon you…" (1:8).

The means by which God's kingdom will be extended is a life-changing encounter with the Holy Spirit. Jesus's ministry began with an encounter with the Holy Spirit (Mk 1:9–13). The church began its ministry with a life-changing encounter with the Holy Spirit (Acts 2:1–4).

According to Joel's prophecy, this life-changing experience with the Holy Spirit is to continue throughout that time called "the last days" (plural). That time between Christ's ascension and return. Peter confirmed this experience in Acts 2:39.

3. THE METHOD. 1:8, 2:17–47

There are four parts to the method Jesus prescribed for His church.

(1) Geographically focused (1:8)

(2) God-centered (2:22–36)

(3) Gospel-accurate (2:37–39)

(4) Church-oriented (2:40–47)

The method prescribed by Jesus and used by the church produced the following results:

(a) A new affection (2:40)

(b) A new allegiance (2:41)

(c) A new alignment (2:42–45)

(d) A new assignment (2:45–47)

4. THE MANNER. 1:14

"These all continued in one accord in prayer and supplication…" (2:14).

A new decorum was introduced. The church was in one accord—they were unanimously harmonious. The church continued in prayer until the day of Pentecost. To continue the ministry of Jesus the church must continue in prayer.

"Men may spurn our appeals, reject our message, oppose our arguments, despise our persons…but they are helpless against our prayers." (**Sidlow Baxter)**

In the pursuit to continue the ministry of Jesus, let us not fail to remember Christ's final instructions.

30

The Lord of Heaven's Armies
Zechariah 8:1–23 NLT

The prophets Haggai and Zechariah have been summoned to a people whose vision has stalled. Sixteen years earlier, the returning exiles laid the foundation of the temple with great zeal, only to have their enemies succeed in bringing the work to a sudden halt. Haggai and Zechariah come with a word from the Lord of heaven's armies.

"The Lord of heaven's armies says" is a phrase repeated some thirteen times in the eighth chapter of Zechariah. A word from God changes everything. A single word from God will rekindle the fire of vision and regain lost momentum.

The Lord of heaven's armies says:

1. THE TASK MAY APPEAR IMPOSSIBLE FOR YOU, BUT IS IT IMPOSSIBLE FOR ME? (8:1–8)

"All this may seem impossible to you now, a small remnant of God's people. But is it impossible for me? says the Lord of heaven's armies" (8:6).

The Lord of heaven's armies is passionate and strong toward his people and his work. He will show himself strong on behalf of his people.

2. BE STRONG AND FINISH THE TASK! (8:9–17)

"Be strong and finish the task! Ever since the laying of the foundation of the Temple of the Lord of Heaven's armies, you have heard what the prophets have been saying about completing the Temple..." (8:9).

"Now I will rescue you and make you both a symbol and a source of blessing. So don't be afraid. Be strong, and get on with rebuilding the Temple!" (8:13).

- They had no money (due to high unemployment)
- They had few people (due to the remoteness and danger of the area)
- They had no peace (there were constant controversies, conflict, and conspiracy against the work)

God promised to provide the three essentials of a successful effort—*People, Prosperity, and Peace.* They would become a symbol and source of blessing—a complete reversal of their situation (see Zech 8:11–13).

3. PRIOR SEASONS OF MOURNING WILL BECOME SEASONS OF CELEBRATION. (8:18–19)

"The traditional fasts and times of mourning you have kept...will become festivals of joy and celebration for the people...So love truth and peace" (8:19).

The four fast days commemorated four tragic events in Jewish history: (1) the siege of Jerusalem; (2) the breaching of the walls of

Jerusalem; (3) the destruction of the temple and Jerusalem; (4) the murder of Gedaliah, whom the King of Babylon made governor of Jerusalem. These periods of mourning will be turned into seasons of joy and celebration.

4. YOUR INFLUENCE WILL EXTEND BEYOND YOUR BORDERS. (8:20–23)

> "Many people and powerful nations will come…to seek the Lord of heaven's armies and to ask for his blessings" (8:22).

So hear what the Lord of heaven's armies says and **FINISH THE WORK** He assigned you.

30

Stop Worrying—Start Believing
Isaiah 7:1–25 NLT

"The news had come to the royal court of Judah; 'Syria is allied with Israel against us...'" (7:2).

The response to the news of this threat speaks volumes. "The hearts of the king and his people trembled with fear, like trees shaking in a storm" (7:2).

No leader wants to hear "A coalition of opposition has developed and they're gunning for you!"

The prophet Isaiah speaks to leaders and people who are facing such a situation, whether real or imagined.

1. STOP WORRYING. (7:4)

"Tell him to stop worrying. Tell him he doesn't need to fear the fierce anger of these two burned-out embers..." (7:4).

Worry, fear, and unbelief cause wavering and vacillating. You can't believe and squirm in fear at the same time. "Be careful, be quiet, do not fear, do not let your heart be faint" (7:4 ESV).

Ahaz and the Lord had different views concerning the threat. Ahaz had placed his trust in the king of Assyria (2 Kings 16:1–9).

> "It is better to trust in the Lord than to put confidence in man. It is better to trust in the Lord than to put confidence in princes" (Ps 118:8–9 NKJ).

2. START BELIEVING. (7:9)

> "Unless your faith is firm, I cannot make you stand firm" (7:9).

Human threats are to be dismissed and divine promise firmly trusted. If you're not firm in your faith, you will not be firm at all. Fear destabilizes, but faith enables you to stand confidently. Whatever has your focus has your faith. Whatever has your focus has your future.

"God's word goes to work when we believe it and stand on it in faith. Faith in God, not faith in man, gives the victory." (**Warren Wiersbe**)

> "Listen to Me, all ye people of Judah and Jerusalem! Believe in the Lord your God and you will be able to stand firm. Believe his prophets, and you will succeed" (2 Chron 20:20 NLT).

3. ASK FOR CONFIRMATION. (7:10–12)

"Later, the Lord sent this message to King Ahaz: 'Ask the Lord your God for a sign of confirmation...' But the king refused. 'No' he said, 'I will not test the Lord like that'" (7:10–12 NLT).

Some time had lapsed following the initial word spoken to Ahaz. Apparently the vacillating continued, so the Lord offered a "sign of confirmation." To confirm means to strengthen, to remove doubt by authoritative statement or action (definition NLT).

"Ahaz pretended to be spiritual when he refused to ask a sign, but his rejection of the sign was actually a rejection of the Lord and His messenger." **(Warren Wiersbe)**

Ahaz had set his heart to reject God's help and to place his trust in the king of Assyria to deliver him.

The need for a sign is an indication that Ahaz was still vacillating between fear and faith. A humble person would have seen and accepted the offer of a sign as the mercy of the Lord. In pride Ahaz refused the Lord's offer.

Whether the leader is filled with fear or faith, both are contagious. The people will eventually catch one or the other.

"Keep your fears to yourself, share your courage with others." **(Robert Louis Stevenson)**

32

The God Who Hides Himself
Isaiah 45:15

"Truly you are God, who hides yourself, O God of Israel, the Savior."

"How long, O lord? Will you forget me forever? How long will You hide Your face from me?" (PS 13:1).

"And do not hide Your face from Your servant, for I am in trouble, hear me speedily" (Ps 69:17).

1. WHY GOD HIDES HIMSELF.

"It is the glory of God to conceal a matter, but the glory of kings is to search out a matter." (Prov 25:2)

God hides himself because of his infinite worth.

God has promised never to leave us, but he does hide himself so that we may value his worth. In Christ are hidden all the treasures of wisdom and knowledge (Col 2:3). Moses cried, "Show me your glory" (Ex 33:17). He had already seen a great deal of God and desired more. God shares himself with those who value him (Mt 7:6–7).

God hides himself that we may desire more of him.

Familiarity breeds contempt, but absence makes the heart grow fonder. *"And I will wait on the Lord, who hides His face from the house of Jacob; and I will hope in Him" (Is 8:17).*

2. WHEN GOD HIDES HIMSELF WE SEEK FOR HIM.

> "For he who comes to God must believe that He is, and that He is a rewarder of those who diligently seek Him" (Heb 11:6).

The Lord reveals Himself to the diligent seeker. The word "diligent" means: carefully, constantly, with perseverance, not the complacent and content, but the hungry, thirsty, and desperate.

When we seek the Lord diligently, it demonstrates the value we place on His person. "Again, the Kingdom of Heaven is like a treasure hidden in a field, which a man found and hid; and for joy over it goes and sells all that he has and buys that field" (Mt 13:44). Jesus is the "treasure" in the field. He is of infinite worth and value, and for joy we sell everything that formerly appeared of worth to have Him. The more we see of Christ the more valuable He is to us.

3. WHEN WE SEEK FOR HIM WE FIND HIM.

> "Then you will call upon Me and go and pray to Me, and I will listen to you, and you will seek Me and find Me when you seek for Me with all your heart" (Jer 29:12–13).

When we call—God listens. When we seek Him we find Him (Mt 7:7). God will withdraw His conscious presence to see if He is valued enough to be pursued. When He is pursued, he reveals himself in greater measure.

"When thou prayest, rather let thy heart be without words than thy words be without heart." **(John Bunyon)**

33

Hopeless Without the Spirit
Acts 1:1–8

The mission of the church will not be realized in the hands of a people without a vital relationship with the Holy Spirit.

Eight truths concerning the Holy Spirit appear in the first two chapters of Acts.

1. THE HOLY SPIRIT IS A PERSON.

Jesus used personal pronouns when referring to the Holy Spirit (Jn 14:17). The Holy Spirit is a real person, not an impersonal force. He shares all the attributes and prerogatives of the Godhead. He is equal in essence with the Father and the Son.

2. THE HOLY SPIRIT IS A PRIORITY.

"Wait for the promise of the father..." (Acts 1:4).

All nonessential activity is to cease so that priority may be given to the pursuit of the Holy Spirit. "Wait," or "tarry" in the KJV, means: to delay, linger, to stay for a time, especially longer than originally intended. To stay until.

3. THE HOLY SPIRIT IS TO BE PURSUED.

Once He is the priority then the church is to pursue Him in earnest prayer.

> "These all continued with one accord in prayer and supplication..." (Acts 1:14).

4. THE HOLY SPIRIT IS A PROMISE.

The promise extends beyond the first generation of disciples to all believers in every generation and dispensation; regardless of age, gender, or economic status.

> "For the promise is to you and to your children, and to all who are afar off, as many as the Lord our God will call" (Acts 2:39).

5. THE HOLY SPIRIT IS A PARENTAL PROMISE.

> "Wait for the promise of the father..." (Acts 1:4). "The promise of the father is for all his children" (Lk 11:13, Jn 20:17). "The promise of the father is the Baptism of the Holy Spirit. An endowment of power." (Acts 1:4–5, Lk 24:49).

6. THE HOLY SPIRIT PROMISE IS PERSONAL.

Seven times in Acts 1:4–8 the pronoun "you" is used to emphasize the personal nature of the experience.

> "They were all filled with the Holy Spirit—each of them" (Acts 2:3–4).

7. THE HOLY SPIRIT IS FOR POWER.

"But you shall receive power when the Holy Spirit has come upon you…" (Acts 1:8).

The power is for our weakness, witness, worship, and our work.

8. THE HOLY SPIRIT HAS A PURPOSE.

"You shall be witnesses to me…" (Acts 1:8).

When believers are filled with the Holy Spirit they are witnesses with power from on high.

"If we don't have spiritual power, how can we accomplish what needs to be done?" **(Jim Cymbala,** *Spirit Rising*)

34

The Wind of the Spirit
Acts 2:2

"And suddenly there came a sound from heaven, as of a rushing mighty wind, and it filled the whole house where they were sitting."

Five truths emerge from the second chapter of Acts relating to "the wind of the Spirit."

1. THE WIND OF CHANGE. Acts 2:1–4

"Everything continues in a state of rest unless it is compelled to change by forces impressed upon it." **(Isaac Newton)**

The wind of the Holy Spirit is the force used to compel change in Christ's church. Pentecost ushered in a new day and a new way of God's dealing with man.

"Some people are thrilled by change, others are threatened by change." **(John Piper)**

2. THE WIND OF CONTROVERSY. Acts 2:5–39

"No great advance has been made in science, politics or religion without controversy." **(Lyman Beecher)**

The disciples, like Jesus, expected and embraced controversy. They viewed it as inevitable, essential, even desirable.

The crowd on the day of Pentecost was confused (2:6), amazed (2:7), marveled (2:7), perplexed and mocking (12–13). The disciples had a fivefold response to the controversy.

- They stood up. (2:14)
- They spoke up. (2:14–15)
- They opened up. The scripture. (2:16–21)
- They lifted up. Jesus. (2:22–36)
- They offered up. The promise. (2:37–39)

Controversy *always* precedes change. Without controversy there is *no* significant change.

3. THE WIND OF COURAGE. Acts 2:36–38

The wind of the Holy Spirit changed this band of disciples from cowards locked away in the upper room out of fear to a courageous people confronting the culture of their day with a fearless proclamation of the gospel of Jesus Christ.

> "Now when they saw the boldness of Peter and John, and perceived that they were uneducated and untrained men, they marveled, and they realized that they had been with Jesus" (Acts 4:13).

> "The ultimate measure of a man is not where he stands in moments of comfort and convenience, but where he stands at times of challenge and controversy." **(Dr. Martin Luther King, Jr.)**

"When the church stands up for and with God she will discover God has already stood up with and for her" *(*Acts 7:55–56).

4. THE WIND OF CONVICTION. (Acts 2:36–39)

When Peter spoke the multitude cried out, their heart lacerated by the wind of the Holy Spirit upon the words Peter spoke. Peter called them to repentance, remission of sins, and reception of the Holy Spirit.

"Many people use mighty thin thread when mending their ways." **(Unknown)**

5. THE WIND OF COMMUNITY. (Acts 2:40–47)

"The Holy Spirit creates community. He baptizes into the body of Christ" (1 Cor 12:13).

Those who believed were added to the church. There is no such thing as a spirit-filled believer who has no relationship to the local church.

"All who believed were together" (Acts 2:44).

If you are led by the Holy Spirit, He will connect you to a local church.

"A man who isolates himself seeks his own desire; he rages against all wise judgment" (Prov 18:1).

"The wind is blowing again
The wind is blowing again
Just like the day of Pentecost
The wind is blowing again"
Song Lyrics

35

The Church and the Gospel
Philippians 1:1–30 NLT

A.B. Simpson is reported to have said that the gospel "Tells rebellious men that God is reconciled, that justice is satisfied, that sin has been atoned for, that the judgment of the guilty may be revoked, the condemnation of the sinner cancelled, the curse of the Law blotted out, the gates of hell closed, the portals of heaven opened wide, the power of sin subdued, the guilty conscience healed, the broken heart comforted, the sorrow and misery of the Fall undone. (*Evangelism*, **M. Cocoris**, *A Biblical Approach*)

1. THE CHURCH IS BIRTHED BY THE GOSPEL.

> "And I am certain that God, who began the good work within you, will continue His work until it is finally finished on the day when Christ Jesus returns" (Phil 1:6 NLT).

The church is started and sustained by the preaching of the gospel. Where the word of God is preached, the true church is gathered and the false church scattered. God births and builds His church through preaching.

2. THE CHURCH IS TO SPREAD THE GOSPEL.

"For you have been my partners in spreading the good news about Christ from the time you first heard it until now" (Phil 1:5 NLT).

When the gospel is shared, the number of believers will greatly increase (Acts 6:7 NLT). The gospel must be shared to be effective. Those who hear and believe are saved. Pastor and parishioners partner to spread the gospel (Acts19:20).

3. THE CHURCH IS TO DEFEND AND CONFIRM THE GOSPEL.

"You share with me the special favor of God, both in my imprisonment and in defending and confirming the truth of the good news" (Phil 1:7b NLT).

To "defend" the gospel is to respond to accusation or criticism by giving a rational, logical explanation; to answer all questions clearly and accurately. To "confirm" is to strengthen, to give assurance, to remove doubt, to cause to become steadfast, to be established in the certainty of faith (Acts 1:1–3).

4. THE CHURCH IS TO LIVE WORTHY OF THE GOSPEL.

"Above all, you must live as citizens of heaven, conducting yourselves in a manner worthy of the good news about Christ" (Phil 1:27 NLT).

"Few things are harder to put up with than the annoyance of a good example." (**Mark Twain**)

The greatest witness to the truth of the gospel is to be an example worth following. Our life may be the only Bible some will ever read.

"A man's life is always more forcible than his speech." (**C.H. Spurgeon**)

5. THE CHURCH SHOULD STRIVE (FIGHT) FOR THE FAITH OF THE GOSPEL.

> "I will know that you are standing together with one spirit and one purpose, fighting together for the faith, which is the good news.—We are in this struggle together..." (Phil 1:27, 30).

The church is not striving against those outside the church but false teaching within the church (Jude 3,4 NLT). We fight to preserve the gospel.

"Early modernists were not trying to hit at the core of Biblical faith, they were simply trying to make Christianity more palatable to a cynical world.—No church can remain healthy for long if the pulpit is not strong, and no pulpit is truly strong if the Bible is not the basis of the preaching." **(John MacAuthor, Jr,** *Ashamed of the Gospel, p.23; 87***)**

36

God Exceeds the Need

As I walked across the parking lot of my bank, I noticed a single penny on the pavement. Almost without breaking stride, I scooped up the penny and placed it in my empty pocket.

After completing my banking, I drove across town to meet my wife for lunch at a local buffet. When I entered the lobby of the restaurant I encountered a woman counting her money before joining in the line for the buffet. When I approached she looked up and asked, "Excuse me, but do you have a penny?" "Just so happens I do," I said and reached in my pocket, retrieved the lone penny, and gladly gave it to her. Having enough to pay for her lunch, she joined us in the buffet line.

My wife and I learned that the lady was from out of town and had come to our community for a job interview. Following the interview, she stopped for lunch before returning home. As we approached the register, my wife and I both knew we were to buy our new friend's lunch. She was pleasantly grateful.

During lunch and on the drive back to my office, I had the sense that the Lord had a lesson for me to learn from my experience that morning. As I prayed, three truths became crystal clear from the experience.

1. GOD KNOWS THE NEED.

"Jehovah-Jireh" means the Lord sees and provides (Gen. 22:14). God sees our need beforehand and makes provision in advance of the need.

God saw the lady's need before she was even aware a need existed and had provided for her in advance. God knew Abraham was going to need a ram, and He provided one in advance. God enabled Abraham to see the ram caught in the thicket.

God knows the need and He will get the provision to you! He is "Jehovah-Jireh."

2. GOD MEETS THE NEED.

Paul was confident when he said "and my God shall supply all your need according to His riches in glory by Christ Jesus" (Phil 4:19).

When you consider all the people, places, and events that had to synchronize to make the "penny miracle" a reality, you must be impressed with God's goodness, sovereignty, and knowledge that operates in our daily lives.

I never have money on me. I am an ATM guy. The Lord placed a single penny in my path, kept anyone else from retrieving it until I arrived, then had me in the right place at the right time to transfer that single penny to someone who needed it.

If God will work that many details out for a single penny, what lengths must He be willing to go to help in more serious situations. He knew what the need was and He got the provision to her on time.

3. GOD EXCEEDS THE NEED.

To "exceed" is to go beyond, more than or greater than, to surpass, to outdo, to exceed one's expectation to a great degree.

That single penny met the lady's immediate need, and lunch was paid for. However, the Lord wasn't finished blessing her or teaching me. When my wife and I paid for her lunch, God exceeded her need. Her lunch was paid for and enjoyed *and* she left with money in her pocket.

> "Now to Him who is able to do exceedingly abundantly above all that we ask or think, according to the power that works in us" (Eph 3:20).

I can't think of an incident in scripture where God did not exceed the need and expectations of His people. He will do the same for you.

Next time you see a penny on the ground, grab it! It may be your invitation to be part of a miracle of provision. Let this life parable encourage you when you have a need.

37

When God Turns up the Heat
Isaiah 54:16

"Behold, I have created the blacksmith who blows the coals in the fire, who brings forth an instrument for his work..."

Three Truths Appear in This Text

1. GOD CREATES THE HEAT.

"Behold I have created the blacksmith who blows the coals in the fire..."

God creates the heat to purge and purify. Malachi declared, "He will sit as a refiner and fire purifier of silver; He will purify the sons of Levi, and purge them as gold and silver, that they may offer to the Lord an offering in righteousness" (3:3).

The "heat" cannot be avoided. The word of God declares: when, not if, you pass through the fire (Is 43:2) The refining fire of God is for our good, not our harm (1 Pt 1:7).

2. GOD CONTROLS THE HEAT.

"The blacksmith blows the coals in the fire…"

The blacksmith controls the amount of heat by blowing on the coals. The blacksmith can lower or raise the level of heat according to his purposes.

The heat is not random, but controlled. God will not allow the heat to go beyond His purpose. Both the temperature of the fire and the time in the fire is in the control of God. God will never "outsource" his refining work.

3. GOD CREATES WITH THE HEAT.

"Who brings forth an instrument for his work."

God has a work to be done. He needs an instrument shaped specifically for that work. God turns up the heat to turn out an instrument. The instrument becomes a weapon in the hand of God. The word "instrument" is often translated "weapon."

Robert Murray McCheyne wrote to Dan Edwards after the latter's ordination as a missionary. "In great measure, according to the purity and perfections of the instrument, will be the success. It is not great talents God blesses so much as great likeness to Jesus. A holy minister is an awful weapon in the hand of God." (**Paul Borthwick,** *Leading the Way*)

Hebrews 12:5–11 reveals the approach we should take when experiencing the fire of God. Don't despise it (12:5), don't be discouraged by it (12:5), endure it (12:7), understand it (12:8), yield to it (12:9), profit from it (12:10), be trained by it (12:11).

Refiner and Purifier of Silver

Malachi 3:3 says: "He will sit as a refiner and purifier of silver."

This verse puzzled some women in a Bible study and they wondered what this statement meant about the character and nature of God.

One of the women offered to find out the process of refining silver and get back to the group at their next Bible study.

That week, the woman called a silversmith and made an appointment to watch him at work. She didn't mention anything about the reason for her interest beyond her curiosity about the process of refining silver.

As she watched the silversmith, he held a piece of silver over the fire and let it heat up. He explained that in refining silver, one needed to hold the silver in the middle of the fire where the flames were hottest so as to burn away all the impurities.

The woman thought about God holding us in such a hot spot, and then she thought again about the verse that says: "He sits as a refiner and purifier of silver."

She asked the silversmith if it was true that he had to sit there in front of the fire the whole time the silver was being refined.

The man answered that yes, he not only had to sit there holding the silver, but he had to keep his eyes on the silver the entire time it was in the fire. If the silver was left a moment too long in the flames, it would be destroyed.

The woman was silent for a moment. Then she asked the silversmith, "How do you know when the silver is fully refined?" He smiled at her and answered, "Oh, that's easy—when I see my image in it."

"If today you are feeling the heat of the fire, remember that God has His eye on you and will keep watching you until He sees His image in you." **(Author Unknown)**

38

The Power of the Tithe
Malachi 3:6–12

The 700 Club TV segment known as *Bring It On* received this e-mail from a viewer. "My church seems to always be in financial need. Yet, I never hear a message on tithing. Could there be a connection?" The host responded, "Certainly there is a connection. The minister must tell the people about the blessing of giving."

Before someone chimes in with "tithing is old covenant!" read the first five verses of Malachi 3. These verses speak of the ministry of John the Baptist preparing the way for "the messenger of the covenant," Jesus Christ. The book closes with similar references to the New Testament ministry of Jesus. Tithing is presented in the context of new covenant realities. If tithing isn't New Testament, what is Jesus doing receiving tithes? (Heb 7:1–19).

Israel, like God's people in every dispensation, was experiencing the consequences of their failure to bring God's tithe. God calls for His people to return to Him and He will demonstrate to them "the power of the tithe."

1. THE TITHE WILL OPEN WHAT HAD BEEN CLOSED. (3:9, 10, 12)

"I will open for you the windows of heaven…" (3:10).

The windows had been closed but now would be open. God wants His people to make the connection between their closed hand and His closed heaven; their open hand and His open heaven. Abraham made the connection (Gen 14:18–20); Jacob made the connection (Gen 28:10–22). Have you made the connection? (Hag 1:1–4, 2:15–19).

2. THE TITHE WILL RELEASE WHAT HAD BEEN WITHHELD. (3:9–10)

Because the tithe had been withheld, the blessing was also withheld.

Rather than living in an ever-increasing capacity of the blessing, they were living in a diminishing capacity of the curse. The blessing that was being withheld would be restored in response to the bringing of the tithe into the storehouse.

"From this day forward I will bless you" (Hag 2:19).

3. THE TITHE WILL NOT ALLOW WHAT HAD BEEN PERMITTED. (3:11)

The devourer is rebuked in response to the tithe. They would once again enjoy the fruit of their labor. Profitability would be restored. The devourer was diminishing their personal and national assets. This would not continue when the tithe was restored. The profit would not be devoured. The tithe puts God on your side against the devourer.

"I have tried to keep things in my hands and lost them all. But what I have given into God's hands I still possess." (**Martin Luther**)

"Give according to your income, lest God make your income according to your giving." **(Peter Marshall)**

4. THE TITHE WILL ENABLE YOU TO BECOME WHAT YOU COULD NOT APART FROM IT. (3:12)

"God promises that if God's people are faithful in presenting their tithe, then the desperately needed rain would come (v 10). Pestilence and crop failure would cease (v 11). And the Abrahamic promise that all nations will call you blessed will be fulfilled (v 12, Ps 72:17)." **ESV Study Bible,** note on verse 12

39

Money Follows Vision

"And He said to them, 'When I sent you without money bag, knapsack and sandals, did you lack any thing?' so they said, 'nothing'" (Lk 22:35).

FINANCIAL CLIFF OR FINANCIAL LIFT?

Which will it be? According to leadershipnet.org, church offerings and worship attendance actually increased in 2012 in spite of the nation's economic landscape. leadership.net research indicates that 73 percent of churches surveyed expect to meet or exceed their 2012 budgets in 2013. Church leadership must decide for their congregations: "financial cliff or financial lift?"

VISION BEYOND RESOURCES

"We want to give a gift, and there are no strings attached, but before I tell you how much we're going to give, I want to tell you why we're giving it. We're giving the gift because you have a vision beyond your resources—we want to give the church three million dollars." (**Mark Batterson,** *The Circle Maker*)

Most churches don't have a money problem, they have a vision problem. MONEY FOLLOWS VISION.

"People give to causes that flow out of vision. I don't articulate a vision for the sole purpose of raising money, but if I cast vision well, I see money raised." (**Gary Fenton,** *Mastering Church Finances*)

> "The silver is mine, and the gold is mine, says the Lord of hosts" (Hag 2:8).

MONEY FOLLOWS VISION

David had a vision for the building of a temple to house the ark of the covenant. He purchased the land and began to amass the resources to be used in the construction of the temple. He said to his son Solomon:

> "I have worked hard to provide materials for building the temple of the Lord—nearly 4,000 tons of gold, 40,000 tons of silver, and so much iron and bronze it cannot be weighed. I have gathered timber and stone for the walls, though you may need to add more" (1 Chron 22:14 NLT).

At today's prices, the value of four thousand tons of gold is approximately 217,600,000 dollars. The silver is worth approximately 448,000,000 dollars. This massive amount doesn't include what David and the leaders contributed in silver, gold, iron, and bronze. They gave an additional 308 tons of gold, ten thousand gold coins, 640 tons of silver, 675 tons of bronze and 3,750 tons of iron (1 Chron 29:4–8).

> "The people rejoiced over the offerings, for they had given freely and wholeheartedly to the Lord, and King David was filled with joy" (1 Chron 29:9).

The point of the story—MONEY FOLLOWS VISION. Current resources should not be allowed to determine the size of your vision. Let your vision determine the size of your resources. Money will follow vision.

"If God be your partner—plan BIG," says D.L. Moody. God's vision will have God's provision. TONS OF IT!

40

Be There
Exodus 24:12–18

Then the Lord said to Moses, "Come up to Me on the mountain and **be there**…" (12*)*.

1. THE CALL TO BE THERE. (12)

"Be there" is a personal summons. Moses is called to meet with God for a personal mountain summit. He is to be there without anyone with him, waiting for God to come.

"Be there" alone, when nothing is happening, so you will be there when everything is happening.

"Be there" until I come. Be there without Me, be there wanting Me, be there waiting for Me—separate from others.

"Be there" hungry, tired, alone, cold, isolated away from all distractions and demands.

"Be there" in silence and submission, waiting for Me. Be there, I am coming to meet you. Don't leave, I will be there and you won't be disappointed.

2. THE CHOICE TO BE THERE. (13)

> "So Moses arose...and Moses went up to the mountain of God" (13).

The choice to be there is our personal choice. The choice we make will directly impact many lives. It is hard to come apart, to separate from all the activities and demands of life.

Leaders are called to lead from the overflow of having been there. We gain so much when we are there and lose so much when we fail to be there.

The choice to be there or not to be there is our personal choice. A choice made with struggles and conflict. Jesus informed His men, "The spirit is willing, but the flesh is weak" (Mt 26:41). **Be there** anyway.

3. THE CONSEQUENCES OF BEING THERE. (15–16)

> "Then Moses went up to the mountain, and a cloud covered the mountain. Now the glory of the Lord rested on Mount Sinai, and the cloud covered it for six days, and on the seventh day He called to Moses out of the midst of the cloud" **(15–16).**

God wants you to **be there**, because He is going to show up— show out and show you things you would not otherwise see.

Moses waited for six days before God showed up on the seventh day. For forty days God revealed His plans for the tabernacle and all its many details. Moses was shown the priesthood and the garments to adorn the priest. Moses was given principles and precepts to guide the nation. He received the Ten Commandments written by the finger of God. Moses shone with the glory of God. The people could not look upon him. He concealed the glory with a veil over his face.

God has so much to show his people (1Cor 1:9–11; Jer 33:3). So much that He wants to do with His church. God is looking for a people who will separate themselves. Come apart to the mountain to **be there** with Him, waiting for Him, hungry for Him, willing to be alone with Him.

When anyone chooses to be there, God will show up and show out for His glory and our good. **Be there!** Alone if necessary, but **be there**. Be the conduit of God's message and direction for His people.

BE THERE, you won't be disappointed.

41

Money for Ministry
2 Corinthians 9:8

"And God is able to make all grace abound toward you, that you, always having all sufficiency in all things, may have an abundance for every good work" (9:8).

Money is critical for ministry!

When the money is there the Moral is up.

When the money is there the Momentum is up.

When the money is there the Motivation is up.

When the money is there the Mandate is up. **(John Maxwell)**

Three crucial questions regarding money for ministry are answered in our scripture text.

1. WHERE DOES MONEY FOR MINISTRY COME FROM?

The source of money for ministry is God Himself. "God is able to make all grace abound toward you…" God supplies money for ministry according to "His riches in glory" (Phil 4:19).

"There is little doubt that "all grace" refers to such a supply that there is no need outside the reaches of its riches. God is the source of our total supply, and God owns all the wealth of every kind in every realm. It is not too much to suppose that the term "all grace" is an all-inclusive term. We would not be amiss to say that God's grace involves all God has, all God has done, and all God is!" (**Jack Taylor,** *God's Miraculous Plan of Economy*)

2. HOW MUCH MONEY FOR MINISTRY CAN ONE EXPECT TO RECEIVE?

The answer is: an abundance. "God is able to make all grace abound toward you, that you, always having all sufficiency in all things, may have an abundance for every good work" (2 Cor 9:8).

God's grace abounding toward you will give "all sufficiency" (more than the need), at "all times" in "all things."

God Exceeds the Need!
Ephesians 3:20

God is able to <u>do</u> what we ask or think.

God is able to do <u>all</u> we ask or think.

God is able to do <u>above</u> all we ask or think.

God is able to do <u>abundantly</u> above all we ask or think.

God is able to do <u>exceedingly</u>, abundantly above all we ask or think.

3. WHAT IS THE PREREQUISITE FOR RECEIVING MONEY FOR MINISTRY?

God will supply abundantly for "every good work." A "good" work is God's work, a work initiated by God and existing for God's glory.

"Here are some guidelines for evaluating a good work. The work must have been initiated by the Lord; the work must be redemptive in nature; the work must exist to God's glory, not men's; the work must have as its purpose to exalt Jesus Christ in everything." **(Jack Taylor,** *God's Miraculous Plan of Economy***)**

"An abundance for every good work is the promise God makes. We are responsible for assuring our work qualifies as a "good work." **(Jack Taylor)**

Leaders are responsible for the cash flow of the church. How well we lead in this area speaks volumes concerning our leadership. Failure here spells disaster elsewhere. Finances are the first place to establish leadership credibility.

42

The Buy-In
1 Chronicles 13:1–14

"People don't at first follow worthy causes, they follow worthy leaders who promote worthy causes. People buy in to their leader first, then the leader's vision." **(John Maxwell)**

The people of Israel have bought in to David, making him their king. Now David needs them to buy in to his vision of returning the ark to Jerusalem and the center of Israel's life and worship. How David proceeds to secure "the buy-in" is a worthy study.

1. DAVID CONSULTED WITH HIS LEADERS.

> "Then David consulted with the captains of thousands and hundreds, and with every leader" (13:1).

Leaders are the first level of the buy-in. David consulted with his leaders at every level. Leaders of thousands, hundreds, all his leaders. Once the leaders are on board, they will use their influence to secure support for the vision. Securing the "buy-in" from your leaders first will save your "good idea" from getting shot down later.

David consulted with his leaders. This was a dialogue with them, not a monologue from David. Webster defines "consult" as: to talk things over, to seek an opinion from—in order to decide or plan something.

2. DAVID SPOKE TO THE PEOPLE.

> "And David said to all the assembly of Israel, 'if it seems good to you, and if it is of the Lord our God,…let us bring the ark of our God back to us.—Then all the assembly said that they would do so, for the thing was right in the eyes of all the people" (13:2–4).

David's vision had become the vision of the people. David secured the "buy-in" from the people. "The thing was right in the eyes of the people." The message people receive is always filtered through the messenger who delivers it.

"People want to go along with people they get along with." **(John Maxwell)**

3. DAVID FAILED TO CONSULT THE LORD.

The project began with great fervor (13:7–8) but failed to have God's favor. Why? David discovered the answer three months after the first attempt met with disaster (13:9–12).

> "For because you did not do it the first time, the Lord our God broke out against us, because we did not consult Him about the proper order" (1 Chron 15:13).

Leaders, especially strong leaders, must exercise caution and be certain they have received "the proper order" for proceeding with a project. How things are done can be as important as what is being done. Once David corrected his mistake, the project ended successfully.

"So David, the elders of Israel, and the captains over thousands went to bring up the ark of the covenant of the Lord from the house of Obed-Edom with joy" (15:25).

Obedience restored favor to the project and joy to the people. The joy of a good thing done right.

43

How to "Vet" a Potential Leader
1 Chronicles 12:1–40 NLT

To "vet" means to examine, evaluate, and investigate expertly. The warriors who were allowed to join and lead David's army serve as a template for evaluating potential leaders. David's men were:

1. BRAVE.

"For they were all brave and able warriors who became commanders of his army" (12:21).

Leadership is not for the faint of heart. You certainly don't want to go to war with the cowardly (Judges 7:3). Leaders must be fearless, not fearful (2 Tim 1:6–12). Joshua was instructed three times "Be strong and of good courage" (Josh 1:6,7,9).

2. SKILLED.

David's men were not only brave—they were skilled warriors (12:8). "All of them were expert archers, and they could shoot arrows or sling stones with their left hand as well as their right" (12:2).

I am known to quip: "I can do more with an inexperienced novice than I can with an expert rebel." While this is a true statement, it is not all the truth on the subject. A great deal can be said for having skilled people to serve with you. David was not the only skilled warrior in his army—this would prove tragic.

3. EXPERIENCED.

The men with David "were brave and experienced men" (12:8). Experience refines one's skills from theoretical to practical.

> "These warriors from Gad were army commanders. The weakest among them could take on a hundred regular troops, and the strongest could take on a thousand" (12:14). WOW.

4. LOYAL.

David personally challenged the potential leaders who were gathering to him. He met them and said:

> "If you have come in peace to help me, we are friends, but if you have come to betray me to my enemies when I am innocent, then may the God of our ancestors see it and punish you" (12:17).

David expected loyalty from all his "warrior leaders." Only after they pledged their loyalty did David allow them to join his ranks.

> "So David let them join him, and he made them officers over his troops" (12:18).

5. COMMITTED.

These "warrior leaders" were committed to David's success and wellbeing. "We are on your side, son of Jesse, peace and prosperity be with you, and success to all who help you, for your God is the one who helps you" (12:18).

"They were all eager to see David become king instead of Saul, just as the Lord had promised" (12:23).

6. SPIRITUAL.

These "warrior leaders" were men of the spirit. "Then the spirit came upon Amasai, the leader of the thirty…" (12:18).

When "vetting" potential leaders, we must look for men and women of the spirit. "Spiritual" leaders will influence by the spirit. "Carnal" leaders will have a carnal influence. "Filled with the Holy Spirit" is still a priority when searching for leaders. "Select seven men who are well respected and are full of the Holy Spirit and wisdom…" (Acts 6:3 NLT).

7. JOYFUL.

"There was great joy throughout the land of Israel" (12:40). The fruit of properly vetted leaders is a joyful people, healthy and celebrating (12:38–40). Failure to properly vet leaders will give access to those with an Absalom spirit (2 Sam 15–18). Protect your people and ministry—expertly vet your potential leaders.

44

God Is in the Details
Matthew 17:24–27

Peter is instructed to catch a fish and to pay the temple taxes with the money found in its mouth. What are the odds of this actually occurring? Think about it.

The Miracle

A single fisherman	standing in a single place
A single fishing line	a single moment in time
A single hook	catching a single fish

Recovering a single coin

A British man lost his cell phone at sea; it was later found and returned to him. Strange coincidence, but no miracle.

The Meaning

A sovereign and almighty God orders the details of His world and ours. Christ is demonstrating ownership, lordship, and sufficiency in His world and ours. God is in the details!

He is All-Knowing

Christ knew Peter's concern about the temple taxes and anticipated his questioning. God is all-knowing. God knows in advance and provides in advance. This is the meaning of Jehovah-Jireh. God sees before and provides before. God is in the details. He knows every detail in His world and ours. He always knows what He is going to do (Jn 6:6).

> "Your father knows the things you have need of before you ask Him" (Mt 6:8).

He is All-Powerful

In order to control and direct His world and ours, God must be all-powerful. If a greater power existed, He might be hindered in His control. There is no such power in existence (Eph 1:15–23).

> "God has spoken once, twice I have heard this: that power belongs to God" (Ps 62:11).

He is All-Sufficient

He is more than enough. His disciples were encouraged to remember the feeding of the five thousand and four thousand, and how much remained after all were filled (Mt 16:9–10). This reality will strengthen faith in Christ's sufficiency.

The Message

Matthew, the tax collector, was fascinated by this miracle. When we are in seemingly impossible situations, God is in the details. God orders His world and ours to make miracle provision available to His people. Compare your situation to this extreme case and be encouraged: God is in the details—obey him no matter how bizarre it seems.

45

The Place of Blessing
Genesis 26:1–33

"Dwell in this land, and I will bless you—so Isaac dwelt in Gerar" (26:3,6).

Like Isaac, our blessing is personal and geographical. God cares where we live and serve. Isaac dwelt in Gerar—"annoyance." His place of blessing came disguised as a place of "annoyance." His circumstances were contradicting his promise. He was experiencing: famine (26:1), fear (26:7), failure (26:7), fighting (26:15,20,21), and frustration (26:13,21). Isaac did three things and turned his annoyances into blessings.

1. HE STAYED IN THE LAND. (2–6)

The promises made to Isaac for remaining in the land were personal, generational, and global. Momentary circumstances should not be allowed to cause us to miss out on God's promised blessing. Long-term solutions (leaving) should not be applied to short-term problems.

Isaac turned his annoyances into blessings by persevering and staying in the land.

From the diary of John Wesley:

Sunday. A.M. May 6 Preached in St. Anne's. Was asked not to come back anymore.

Sunday, P.M. May 6 Preached in St. John's. Deacons said "Get out and stay out."

Sunday, A.M. May 12 Preached in St. Jude's. Can't go back there either.

Sunday, A.M. May 19 Preached in St. Somebody Else's. Deacons called special meeting and said I couldn't return.

Sunday, P.M. May 19 Preached on street. Kicked off street.

Sunday, A.M. May 26 Preached in meadow. Chased out of meadow as bull was turned loose during service.

Sunday, A.M. June 2 Preached out at the edge of town. Kicked off the highway.

Sunday, P.M. June 2 Afternoon, preached in a pasture. Ten thousand people came out to hear me. **(John Wesley)**

2. HE SOWED IN THE LAND. (26:12–13)

"Then Isaac sowed in that land, and reaped in the same year a hundred fold, and the Lord blessed him. The man began to prosper, and continued to prosper until he became very prosperous." (26:12–13)

Sowing in difficult times may prove more significant than what appears to be more favorable conditions. Isaac sowed to his future rather than reacting to his present. He also dug wells in the land.

There are seven references to digging wells in our scripture text.

> "And let us not grow weary while doing good, for in due season we shall reap if we do not lose heart" (Gal 6:9).

"Nothing in this world can take the place of persistence. Talent will not; nothing is more common than unsuccessful men with talent. Genius will not; unrewarded genius is almost a proverb. Education will not; the world is full of educated derelicts. Persistence and determination alone are omnipotent. The slogan "press on" has solved and always will solve the problems of the human race." **(Calvin Coolidge,** in *Bits and Pieces*)

3. HE SACRIFICED IN THE LAND. (26:25)

> "So he built an altar there and called on the name of the Lord, and pitched his tent there; and there Isaacs's servants dug a well" (26:25).

Three times the word "there" appears in verse 25. It was "there" in the place of God that Isaac lived and sacrificed to the God of his father who had appeared to him and established His covenant with him. "There" in that place he sacrificed and served his God.

"The law of sacrifice says 'You must give up to go up'—the law of sacrifice maintains that one sacrifice seldom brings success. Sacrifice is an ongoing process, not a onetime payment." **(John Maxwell,** *21 Laws of Leadership*)

"God is ready to assume full responsibility for the life wholly yielded to him." **(Andrew Murray)**

46

The Leader as Messenger
2 Timothy 3:1–17

The Christian leader is first and foremost a messenger. (Jn 1:6–7)

1. AS A MESSENGER THE LEADER MUST KNOW THE TIMES. (3:1)

> "But know this, that in the last days perilous times will come" (3:1).

A. These are the last times.

B. These are perilous times.

C. These are grace times.

D. These are the church's times.

The word perilous means dangerous, hard to deal with, savage, furious, and violent. Against this backdrop this is an age of grace. God is demonstrating His great love for the vilest of sinners.

2. AS A MESSENGER THE LEADER MUST KNOW THE CULTURE. (3:2–7)

Mark J. Bubeck in his book, *The Satanic Revival,* categorizes nineteen characteristics of the culture in the last days. Mark states, "The culture will become demonized much like that of an individual who is demonized."

As a messenger the leader must evaluate the culture through the lens of scripture. There is no fundamental difference between the first and the twenty-first century. Love for the culture requires an accurate assessment of the condition of the culture.

3. AS A MESSENGER THE LEADER MUST KNOW THE CURE. (3:8–17)

As a messenger, the leader has a twofold responsibility to declare the cure for cultural degeneration and to keep believers from being culturized by the very culture they seek to transform.

A. Turn away from the false. (3:5–9)

B. Follow those who are true. (3:10–12)

C. Continue in the word of God. (3:13–17)

Evil men will wax worse, but those who follow the word of God will be safe. The church must seek not only to connect with the culture, but also as messengers to confront the culture in order to transform it. The mandate of the church has not changed. God has called the church to this:

> "To open their eyes, in order to turn them from darkness to light, and from the power of Satan to God, that they may receive forgiveness of sins and an inheritance among those who are sanctified by faith in Me" (Acts 26:18).

47

The Authentic Minister
1 Corinthians 4:1–21

There are four characteristics of an authentic minister and ministry in our text.

1. AN AUTHENTIC MINISTER IS A SERVANT. (4:1)

"Let a man so consider us, as servants of Christ..." (4:1).

The word servant is the word for "under-rower." The lowest deck of a ship was made of single rows on each side. Elevated so all the rowers could see him was the captain of the ship. The rower's task was to row according to the directions of the captain. The captain set the rhythm of the rowers. The rowers rowed at the captain's direction. The minister is an under-rower of Christ, serving at his command and his cadence.

2. AN AUTHENTIC MINISTER IS A STEWARD. (4:2–5)

"Servants of Christ and stewards of the mysteries of God"

(4:1).

A steward is the master of the house. A steward is in charge of the estate in the absence of the owner. The steward represents the interest of the owner. The steward is judged by the owner, not the servants. It is required of stewards to be found faithful (4:2).

3. AN AUTHENTIC MINISTER IS A SPECTACLE. (4:8–13)

> "For we have been made a spectacle to the world, to both angels and to men" (4:9).

Spectacle, *theatron*, is the word for theatre, a place in which games and dramatic spectacles are exhibited. A public show—hence a man who is exhibited to be gazed at and made sport of. An authentic minister must be cautious when all men speak well of him (Lk 6:26). The world will love its own. In seeking to win the world one must not become like the world.

4. THE AUTHENTIC MINISTER IS A SPIRITUAL PARENT. (4:14–21)

> "I do not write these things to shame you, but as my beloved children I warn you" (4:14).

The behavior of the children determines the demeanor of the parent. "Shall I come to you with a rod, or in love and a spirit of gentleness" (4:21). The authentic minister can demonstrate both strength and gentleness. Both are a measured response exercised with restraint and love for the child.

"Nothing is so strong as gentleness and nothing so gentle as real strength." **(Francis de Sales)**

48

Ministry Is a Work of Faith
Mark 11:12–26

"The one common characteristic of successful leaders is faith."
(Elmer Towns)

Faith is essential in ministry. Jesus is instructing the apostles and future leaders in the role of faith in ministry. He demonstrates for them what faith in God will do.

1. FAITH WILL DRY UP WHAT NEEDS TO BE DRIED UP. (11:12–14, 20–22)

"Leaves but no fruit"—religious profession without practice. Faith will dry up those things that do not need to continue to be part of our life and ministry. Faith will cause these things to dry up and wither away.

2. FAITH WILL MOVE WHAT NEEDS TO BE MOVED. (11:22–23)

Obstacles and opposition will be removed to make room for what needs to be (Zech 4:6–7; Lk 3:4–6). Mountains will be made plains to allow the completion of God's purposes.

3. FAITH WILL GET DONE WHAT NEEDS TO BE DONE. (11:23b)

"Believes that those things he says will be done, he will have whatever he says."

The unfinished and the incomplete will be done rather than remain undone. Faith will bring the unfinished to completion.

4. FAITH WILL PROVIDE WHAT YOU DON'T NOW HAVE. (11:24)

"Whatever things you ask when you pray, believe that you receive them, and you will have them."

All things needed will be provided. You will lack nothing required for ministry (Lk 22:35). Everything you don't now have will be provided.

During an especially trying time in the work of the China Inland Mission, Hudson Taylor wrote his wife, "We have twenty-five cents—and all the promises of God." **(Warren Wiersbe)**

5. FAITH WILL ACQUIRE YOUR DESIRE. (11:24 KJV)

"What things soever ye desire, when ye pray, believe that ye receive them, and ye shall have them" (11:24 KJV).

God shares his desires with those who delight in him (Ps 37:4). Desires should not be dismissed or ignored, but prayed for and believed for.

"A man lives by believing something, not by debating and arguing about many things." **(Thomas Carlyle)**

6. FAITH WILL RESTORE RELATIONSHIPS. (11:25–26)

Forgiveness is an act of faith. (See Lk 17:1–5.) It takes faith to let go and let God. It takes faith to lay down an offense. Faith will facilitate restoration of relationships. Forgiveness is fundamental to the Christian faith.

"Not long before she died in 1988—in a moment of surprising candor on television, Marghanita Laski, one of the best known secular humanists, said, 'What I envy most about Christians is your forgiveness, I have nobody to forgive me.'" **(John Stott,** *The Contemporary Christian*)

Conclusion: "God our Father made all things depend on faith so that whoever has faith has everything and whoever does not have faith will have nothing." **(Martin Luther)**

Those called to serve have been given faith equal to their assignment (Rom 12:3; 2 Pt 1:1; 1 Tim 1:14). Faith given is released through: proclamation, petition, and pardon.

"Faith does not operate in the realm of the possible. There is no glory for God in that which is humanly possible. Faith begins where man's power ends." **(George Muller)**

49

The Spirit of the Taker
2 Chronicles 12:1–2

God is a giver—Satan is a taker! (Jn 10:10). Because God is a giver and not a taker, his people are gatherers and not grabbers (Ps 104:27–28). In our text Rehoboam and Israel are experiencing the spirit of the taker.

1. THE SPIRIT OF THE TAKER.

> "In the fifth year of Rehoboam that Shishak king of Egypt came up against Jerusalem…" (12:2)

The name "Shishak" means one who is greedy. A secondary meaning of the name is: "He who gives a drink of water," indicating that the taker will disguise himself as a giver. Proverbs speaks of a host who says to his guests "eat," all the while despising every bite they take. He wants to appear generous, but is actually greedy (Prov 23:6–8).

"Shishak," the taker, took the fortified cities (12:4). He took the treasure of the house of the Lord (12:9). He also took the treasure of the king's house (12:9) . He took the gold shields (12:9). He took everything (12:9). The taker had devastated the nation and the people.

2. HOW THE SPIRIT OF THE TAKER GAINED ACCESS.

> "He (Jeroboam) forsook the law of the Lord, and all Israel along with him" (12:1).

> "And it happened…, because they had transgressed against the Lord" (12:2).

> "You have forsaken me, and therefore I also have left you in the hand of Shishak" (12:5).

Rehoboam and Israel had forsaken the law of the Lord, therefore, they were left in the hands of the taker. To forsake means: to loosen or to relinquish or to leave off. Israel had gotten loose from God and His laws. They threw off the freedom of His ways and encountered the spirit of the taker. The thief takes the word away and the strong man is vulnerable. (See Mk 4:15; Lk 11:21.)

3. HOW TO REMOVE THE SPIRIT OF THE TAKER.

> "Then Shemaiah the prophet came to Rehoboam and the leaders of Judah…so the leaders of Israel and the king humbled themselves, and they said, 'the lord is righteous'" (12:6).

Since pride gave the taker access, humility will close off his access. When we humble ourselves the door is shut to the spirit of the taker. Humility will align you with God against your enemies.

"Therefore, humble yourselves under the mighty hand of God, that he may exalt you in due time...be sober, be vigilant; because your adversary the devil walks about like a roaring lion, seeking who he may devour" (1 Pt 5:6–9).

CONCLUSION: "When he humbled himself, the wrath of the lord turned from him, so as not to destroy him completely; and things also went well in Judah" (12:12).

The result of Jeroboam's realignment was that things went well in Judah. The word "well" means good in the broadest sense. Beautiful, best, graciously, joyfully, kindly, well favored, and prosperous.

"Be humble or you'll stumble." (**D.L. Moody**)

"They that know God will be humble and they that know themselves cannot be proud." (**John Flavel**)

50

The Ministry of Illumination
Exodus 25:37

"You shall make seven lamps for it, and they shall arrange its lamps so they give light in front of it" (Ex 25:37).

1. THE MINISTRY OF THE CHURCH IS A MINISTRY OF ILLUMINATION.

The light must shine bright in God's house. When the light goes out the house goes dark. When the house goes dark all sorts of undesirable things creep in. When the light is bright in God's house, people are drawn to the light. That which is "dark" will be cleansed by the light or repelled by the light.

The church must be careful not to "dim" the light by placing it under a shade (bushel), or to "conceal" the light by hiding it from plain sight (under the bed). Christ and his gospel must occupy a central place (on a lampstand) for all in the house to see. (See Lk 8:16–17). If the light in us (the church) be darkness, how great is that darkness?

2. THE MINISTRY IS A MINISTRY OF ILLUMINATION.

177

"There was a man sent from God, whose name was John. This man came for a witness, to bear witness of the light, that all through him might believe" (Jn 1:6–7).

The priests who ministered in the tabernacle were responsible for cleaning the lamps, replacing the oil, and keeping them burning continually. (See Exodus 27:20, Leviticus 24:2.)

"The preacher is the golden pipe through which the divine oil flows. The pipe must not only be golden but open, that the oil may have a full unhindered, unwasted flow." **(E.M. Bonds,** *Power Through Prayer***)**

- **The ministry illuminates the person of Jesus.**

The priests were instructed to arrange the lampstand so that the light was dispersed in front of the lampstand. Immediately in front of the lampstand was the table of show bread. Literally, "the bread of His face." The word of God reveals the glory of God in the face of Jesus (2 Cor 4:6).

- **The ministry illuminates the way forward.**

"They shall arrange the lamps so they give light in front of it" (Ex 25:37, Num 8:2–3).

The light from the golden candlesticks illuminates the path forward for God's people. Your word is a lamp to my feet and a light to my path (Ps 119:105).

3. EACH CHRISTIAN IS A MINISTRY OF ILLUMINATION.

Illumination occurs when men see the gospel in action. Christians glorify the Father by doing good works that benefit others (Titus 3:14).

"Let your light so shine before men that they may see your good works and glorify your father in heaven" (Mt 5:16).

"I would not give much for your religion unless it can be seen. Lamps do not talk, but they do shine." **(Unknown)**

"A man's life is always more forcible than his speech. When men take stock of him they reckon his deeds as dollars and his words as pennies." **(C.H. Spurgen)**

"Some people change their ways when they see the light, others only when they feel the heat." **(Unknown)**

51

Closing the Door on the Devil
Ephesians 4:25–32

"Nor give place to the devil" Ephesians 4:27

The devil must be given access to our lives and churches; he can't simply take it. Legal right must be given him to have access. Access is gained by attitudes, actions, and words.

We are instructed in the fourth chapter of Ephesians how to deny access to the devil. There are seven things that will close the door to the devil.

1. DEMONSTRATE HONESTY IN RELATIONSHIPS. (4:25)

"Therefore, putting away lying, 'Let each one of you speak truth with his neighbor,' for we are members one of another" (4:25).

2. RESOLVE CONFLICT PROPERLY. (4:26)

"Be angry, and do not sin; do not let the sun go down on your wrath." (4:26)

3. WORK TO CONTRIBUTE. (4:28)

"Let him who stole steal no longer, but rather let him labor, working with his hands what is good, that he may have something to give him who has need" (4:28).

4. SPEAK TO BUILD UP RATHER THAN TO TEAR DOWN. (4:29)

"Let no corrupt word proceed out of your mouth, but what is good for necessary edification, that it may impart grace to the hearers" (4:29).

5. DO NOT GRIEVE THE HOLY SPIRIT. (4:30)

"And do not grieve the Holy Spirit of God, by whom you were sealed for the day of redemption" (4:30).

6. SHOW KINDNESS AND FORGIVENESS RATHER THAN BITTERNESS AND ANGER. (4:31–32)

"Let all bitterness, wrath, anger, clamor, and evil speaking be put away from you, with all malice and be kind to one another, tenderhearted, forgiving one another, even as God in Christ forgave you" (4:31–32).

7. BE ALWAYS BEING FILLED WITH THE SPIRIT. (5:18)

"And do not be drunk with wine, in which is dissipation; but be filled with the spirit" (5:18).

As certain as access is given, access can be revoked. Access is revoked by confession, repentance, and renouncing or revoking Satan's legal right gained by wrong attitudes, actions, and words. Then commanding the devil to leave since his access, his legal rights, have been revoked.

It is worth pointing out that the admonition to "give no place to the devil" is in the context of the corporate life of the church. The

181

instructions must be applied to the corporate body of Christ as well as the individual believer.

> "Be sober, be vigilant; because your adversary the devil walks about like a roaring lion, seeking whom he may devour" (1 Pt 5:8).

The devil is unable to devour those who keep the door to him shut. I recall it being said "When the devil knocks on your door, let Jesus answer." When the church or the Christian becomes loose with their living, failing to be sober and vigilant, they open the door to the devil. Choose rather to slam it in his face.

52

A Mouth Filled with Laughter
Psalm 126:1–6

"When the Lord brought back the captivity of Zion, we were like those who dream. Then our mouth was filled with laughter, and our tongue with singing. Then they said among the nations, 'The Lord has done great things for them'" (126:1–2).

When was the last time you had a good laugh? In the second psalm the Lord of Heaven and earth is revealed as: "Sitting in the heavens and laughing." Have you ever wondered what makes God laugh?

"Why do the nations rage and the people plot a vain thing? The kings of the earth set themselves, and the rulers take council together against the Lord and against His anointed, saying, 'Let us break their bonds in pieces and cast away their cords from us.' He who sits in the heavens shall laugh; the Lord shall hold them in derision" (Ps 2:1–4).

There are many reasons for laughter being a frequent and integral part of our daily lives. We will look at three.

1. LAUGHTER IS THEOLOGICALLY SOUND.

> "When the Lord turned again the captivity of Zion...then our mouth was filled with laughter, and our tongue with singing" (126:1–2).

Laughter is in the Bible. For the Christian, laughter is founded on the redeeming work of Christ. "Therefore, with joy shall you draw water from the wells of salvation" (Is 12:3).

> "Blessed are the people who know the joyful sound! They shall walk, Oh Lord, in the light of your countenance...and in your righteousness they are exalted" (Ps 89:15–16).

God is revealed as the God of Abraham, Isaac, and Jacob. God made Abraham and Sarah laugh (Gen 17:17,18:12). God gave them a son in their old age and had them name him Isaac (laughter).

2. LAUGHTER IS DIAGNOSTICALLY ACCURATE.

"The absence of laughter may be a clear sign of the absence of God. The presence of laughter is an easy sign of the presence of God in one's life. When you find yourself in very serious company where there is *no* place for humor, it is a spiritual warning sign." (*SermonHelp.com*, **Author Unknown**)

"A sour religion is the devil's religion." **(John Wesley)**

Jesus described his ministry as: "Healing the brokenhearted, giving beauty for ashes, the oil of joy for mourning" (Is 61:1–3).

Job was told: "He will yet fill your mouth with laughing, and your lips with rejoicing" (Job 8:21).

> "Blessed are you who weep now; for you shall laugh" (Lk 6:21).

3. LAUGHTER IS THERAPEUTICALLY HEALTHY.

"A merry heart does good, like a medicine. But a broken spirit dries the bones" (Prov 17:22).

"Laughter actually helps free the body of the constricting effects of negative emotions that impair the body's self-healing system." (**Tal D. Bonham**, *Humor: God's Gift*)

A dose of laughter each day can be preventive medicine as well as quicken recovery from illness. Dr. Norman Cousins, suffering from a life-threatening illness reported: "Being pain-free for hours following a few minutes of hearty laughter." (**Dr. Norman Cousins**, *The Anatomy of an Illness*)

"Laughter triggers healthy physical changes in the body. Humor and laughter strengthens your immune system, boosts your energy, diminishes pain and protects you from the damaging effects of pain. Best of all, this priceless medicine is fun, free and easy to use." (www.helpguide.org)

The average child laughs 150 times a day. The average adult, fifteen times a day. Could this be one of the benefits of becoming like a little child to enter the kingdom? (See Mt 18:3.)

53

Jesus Is a People Person
Mark 6:34

"And Jesus, when He came out, saw a great multitude and was moved with compassion for them..." (6:34).

Jesus is a people person! Not because of a sanguine personality, but because He loved and valued people. Jesus "saw" the multitude and was moved with compassion for them. The disciples were often distracted, looking elsewhere. Before the church can minister to the people, she must first "see" the people.

P riority

The first letter in people speaks of the priority Jesus placed on people. Jesus gave priority to people; poor, broken, captive, blind, and oppressed people. (See Lk 4:18,19). Jesus came to seek and save the lost (Mt 18:11). Those who are whole have no need of a physician (Mt 9:12). People are the priority of Jesus's ministry.

E ngaging

"Engaging" is the strategy of Jesus in reaching people. He takes the initiative in engaging people. "And when Jesus came to the place, He looked up and saw him, and said to him: Zacchaeus, make haste and come down, for today I must stay at your house" (Lk 19:5).

"There are two types of people who enter a room—those who say "Here I am!" Others who enter a room and say "There you are!" **(Bob Rhoden,** *Four Faces of a Leader*)

O ptimism

Jesus is optimistic when it comes to people. To be "optimistic" is to take the most helpful and cheerful view. Jesus is hopeful and cheerful when it comes to people (the exception being the legalistic religious crowd). Jesus sees the best in people and brings out the best in them. Optimism draws people to Jesus.

P otential

"Your potential—my priority" would certainly appear in the mission statement of Jesus. Jesus saw the "potential" in people. He empowered people to reach their potential. Jesus could see potential when others failed to see it, even in themselves.

"You were born an original, don't die a copy." **(Author Unknown)**

L ove

Love is the motive of Jesus's ministry. "Greater love has no one than this, than to lay down one's life for his friends" (Jn 15:13). The fruit of Jesus's love is compassion (Eph 2:4). Compassion moves to action. Compassion moved Jesus to action on behalf of people. "He saw a great multitude and was moved with compassion for them…" (Mk 6:34).

E ternal

Jesus viewed people from an eternal perspective. People will last forever. People are of eternal significance. Jesus never built a building, owned a home, or amassed wealth while on earth. He viewed people as the only eternal assets to survive the post-world, time and space continuum. People are the eternal inheritance of Jesus (Eph 1:18).

Jesus saw people and cared for them. He instructed his disciples that to see the harvest, they would have to "lift up their eyes and look" (Jn 4:35).

54

Open Your Mouth Wide
Psalm 81:8–10

"I am the Lord your God, who brought you out of the land of Egypt; Open your mouth wide, and I will fill it" (Ps 81:10).

Three items appear in this verse—the challenge, the commitment, and the choice.

1. THE CHALLENGE.

"Open your mouth wide"

The challenge is personal, open *your* mouth wide. The opening of one's mouth wide speaks of the intensity of desire and the increasing of one's capacity to ask large. God's ability to answer will always exceed our capacity for asking. Opening the mouth wide also speaks of the expectation and anticipation of receiving.

"God is not so much concerned that we will ask too much, but that we will be satisfied with too little." **(John Piper)**

When praying (opening wide your mouth) to a "big God," we should pray "Big Prayers"; this honors God.

2. THE COMMITMENT.

"Open wide your mouth and I will fill it."

To "fill it" means to fully satisfy, completely supply. No matter how large the request, "I will fill it." He satisfies your mouth with good things (Ps 103:5).

When we desire large, God gives lavishly. Expect great things from God—you will not be disappointed. An alternate translation of Ps 81:10 says "Make your request without limit, and I will accede to them all."

"Now to Him who is able to do exceedingly abundantly above all that we ask or think, according to the power that works in us" (Eph 3:20).

3. THE CHOICE.

The challenge is personal: "open wide *your* mouth." The choice is also personal: will you open your mouth wide? "Wide" to express the intensity of desire. "Wide" to express the increasing of your capacity to ask big. "Wide" in expectation and anticipation of receiving.

There is no limit to God's ability—the question is, will we choose to accept the challenge and ask big? (See Mt 7:7–11; Jn 14:13, 15:7–8, 16:23–24).

Scripture is replete with examples of ordinary people who opened wide their mouth. Two Old Testament examples would be Joshua and Jabez. New Testament examples would include the woman with the issue of blood for twelve years. The father whose son was near death and asked Jesus to come and lay hands on his son before he died. Jesus spoke three words and resolved the father's anxiety—"thy son lives."

Three responses can be made to the challenge "open wide your mouth." Some will choose not to open their mouth at all. Others will choose to open their mouth only slightly. Still, there will be those who accept the challenge and choose to open their mouth wide, loud, and long, and they will see great things from God in response.

> "Call to Me, and I will answer you, and show you great and mighty things, which you do not know" (Jer 33:3).

The word "mighty" can be translated "inaccessible," meaning "fenced out" or "cut off." God is able to reveal that which has been formerly hidden, and he is committed to deliver and preserve his people.

Will you accept the challenge and make the choice to take the limits off God by removing the limits to your asking?

NOTE: this Youtube video will help introduce the concept of opening wide your mouth:

www.youtube.com/watch?v=7tugcoYd9fA

55

Against the Odds
2 Chronicles 13:1–22

In the scriptural narrative, Abijah, king of Judah, is fielding 400,000 troops while Jeroboam is fielding 800,000 troops in opposition. The odds are two to one against Abijah and Judah. The odds are against a positive outcome for Abijah. However, Abijah demonstrates four principles that enable him to be victorious "Against the Odds."

1. HE SHOWED UP.

> "When the army of Judah arrived in the hill country of Ephraim" (13:4 NLT).

The first principle for winning against the odds is to show up. When you fail to show up, your enemy wins by default. David showed up and faced Goliath, and it launched him from obscurity to national prominence.

"An enemy arising in your life is an announcement that the next stage of your future is about to be born—God intends for every enemy to be your step stool. The depth of your battle gives you insight into the greatness of your potential—your enemy is unlocking your potential." (**Ron Carpenter Jr.**, *The Necessity of An Enemy*)

2. HE STOOD UP.

> "Then Abijah stood on Mount Zemaraim, which is in the mountains of Ephraim..." (13:4 NKJ).

Abijah knew where he was standing physically. However, more importantly, he knew where he was standing spiritually.
- As a covenant people (13:5)
- On the side of God (13:10)
- Knowing they were living in obedience (13:11)

3. HE SPOKE UP.

> "Then Abijah stood on Mount Zemaraim, which is in the mountains of Ephraim, and said, Hear me, Jeroboam and all Israel..." (13:4).

- He told Jeroboam, you will not defeat "the kingdom of the Lord" (13:8).
- He told Jeroboam, "God himself is with us as our head" (13:12).

4. HE SOLDIERED UP.

> "Then Abijah and his people struck them with a great slaughter; so five hundred thousand choice men of Israel fell slain. Thus the children of Israel were subdued at that time; and the children of Judah prevailed, because they relied on the Lord God of their fathers" (13:17–18).

To the victor go the spoils! Abijah won "Against the Odds." It is interesting to note that Abijah means "God is my Father," while Jeroboam means "his people are countless."

With God as your Father, you can win *"Against the Odds."*

56

A Model Leader
Genesis 50:15–21

Joseph is a model of leadership. "A model" is a standard of excellence to be imitated. Joseph serves as a model of how God goes about raising up a leader and fulfilling destiny.

In grace God often hides the cost involved in fulfilling one's destiny. The leader sees the glory of the dreams fulfilled and rarely the cost involved. Leaders are motivated to pay the price when God reveals the prize.

Joseph is a model leader when it comes to understanding the suffering that shapes the leader. **A.W. Tozer** observed, "God can't use a man until he hurts him deeply." Suffering and hardship is the lot of all would-be leaders.

While there are numerous lessons to observe from Joseph's life as a "model leader," I will call attention to four of them.

1. HIS CONFIDENCE. (50:19–20)

"Joseph said to them, 'Don't be afraid, for am I in the place of God?'" (19).

This is a question, not a statement. Joseph is affirming, "I find myself here by divine providence as do you." God had determined Joseph's place and the route he would take to arrive there. Joseph's confidence comes from knowing God's purpose and plan.

"The Lord directs our steps, so why try to understand everything along the way?" (Prov 20:24 NLT).

"But as for you, you meant evil against me; but God meant it for good, in order to bring it about as it is this day, to save many people alive" (50:20).

2. HIS COMPASSION. (50:16–17)

"Joseph wept when they spoke to him" (17).

R.T. Kendal, in his book, *God Meant It for Good*, says, "Before he could ever be used, Joseph had to come to the place where he loved, where he totally forgave—I believe Joseph wept because he was hurt that they thought he wanted to hurt them."

Joseph was able to be compassionate because he had accepted that it is God's place to execute vengeance and to compensate the victim (Heb 10:30; Rom 12:19). Joseph was far from thinking vengeance, revenge, or retribution; he was compassionate toward his brothers.

3. HIS COMMITMENT. (50:21)

"Do not be afraid; I will provide for you and your little ones…" (21).

The model leader knows that leadership is for the benefit of those they lead. In Colossians 1:24–29, Paul illustrates this truth by showing the ministry is "for you."

The Ministry

Suffers for you (24)
Stewards for you (25)
Strives for you (29)
Speaks for you (28)

Paul concludes the first chapter of Colossians by revealing his passion and purpose for ministry. "That we may present every man perfect in Christ Jesus" (1:28).

4. HIS COMMUNICATION. (50:21)

"And he comforted them and spoke kindly to them" (21) lit; to their heart.

"Everyone spoke well of him and was amazed by the gracious words that came from his lips..." (Lk 4:22 NLT).

"Speaking the truth in love" is how people grow (Eph 4:15). However, truth isn't truth until it is spoken in love. To speak the message of God in a different tone or demeanor than He intended is to distort the message. Truth must be tempered by love. Truth is absolute—the messenger is not.

57

Rules of Engagement
Psalm 63:1–11

Christian leaders and workers experience spiritual warfare. These spiritual assaults vary in size, intensity, and duration. "Rules of Engagement" have been provided in our text to guide our response.

1. REAFFIRM YOUR FAITH. (63:1)

"O God, you are my God!"

The conflict is designed by the enemy to separate you from your faith (Lk 22:31–32). This is an attempt to cut you off from your source of strength that enables you to overcome.

2. RECALL YOUR PAST EXPERIENCES. (63:6–7)

David recalled what God had done for him in the past and meditated on His faithfulness. The recollection built up David's faith and caused him to rejoice in his God.

3. REFUSE TO COMPLAIN. (63:5)

Complaining is counterproductive. There is a difference between complaining and expressing anguish of heart. When we complain, we engage in fault-finding against God. One's attitude at the beginning of a conflict does more to determine the outcome than anything else (63:3–5).

4. RECOGNIZE YOUR WEAPONS. (63:9–10)

> "But those who seek my life, to destroy it, shall go into the lower parts of the earth. They shall fall by the sword; they shall be a portion for jackals" (63:9–10).

Eph 6:17 describes the sword of the spirit. Heb 4:12 declares that the word of God is sharper than any two-edged sword. Rev 1:16 and 19:15 describe the sword coming out of the mouth of Christ. For the sword of the spirit to come out of your mouth, you must first have received the word (Ez 3:1; Ps 8–2).

5. REJOICE IN YOUR ASSURED VICTORY. (63:11)

All who swear by God will triumph. "Now thanks be to God who always leads us in triumph in Christ…" (2 Cor 2:14). "Thanks be to God, who gives us the victory through our Lord Jesus Christ" (1 Cor 15:57). "Yet in all these things we are more than conquerors through Him who loved us" (Rom 8:37).

CONCLUSION:

I'm often asked, "How does one know when they are being attacked?" The Bible describes the kingdom of God within the believer as: righteousness, peace and joy in the Holy Spirit (Lk 17:21; Rom 14:17). You know you are under attack when "your righteousness" from God is being questioned. Satan will seek to undermine your relationship with God. When your righteousness goes, so does your "peace." Peace will be replaced with anxiety. Then your joy, expressed in song, will be absent (Eph 5:18–20). Despair will replace delight.

When you sense these three foundation stones (righteousness, peace, and joy in the Holy Spirit) diminishing, you are likely under attack.

When this occurs, use the "Rules of Engagement" to defeat the enemy and restore tranquility to your life.

58

When Christ is in the House
Mark 2:1–2

When Christ is in the house, whose house we are (Heb 3:6), there are specific things that always accompany Him.

1. THERE IS HIS PRESENCE. (2:1)

"And it was heard that He was in the house" (2:1).

In his book *Becoming a Healthy Church,* **Stephen Macchia** placed God's empowering presence as the number one characteristic of a healthy church. Macchia further stated, "Christ's empowering presence must become a high -value item for the church"

Not every church enjoys Christ's presence. In Rev 3:20, Christ is pictured as outside the church knocking for entry. Will the Church answer?

2. THERE IS PREACHING (2:2)

"And He preached the word to them" (2:2).

Preaching is primary, not secondary!

Thomas Rainer, in his interviews with hundreds of previously unchurched, asked: "Did the pastor and his preaching play a role in your coming to church?" In response, 97 percent answered in the affirmative. (*Surprising Insights From the Unchurched*)

One couple, Frank and Shannon, had this to say about their search for a church. "We attended a lot of different churches for different reasons before we became Christians. I tell you, so many of the preachers spoke with little authority; they hardly ever dealt with tough issues of scripture, and they soft-sold the other issues. Frank and I knew that we were hungry for the truth. Why can't preachers learn that shallow, superficial preaching doesn't help anybody including people like us who were not Christians." (*Surprising Insights*, p. 62)

3. THERE IS PEOPLE (2:2)

"Immediately many gathered together so that there was no longer room to receive them, not even near the door…" (2:2).

People are drawn to the house where there is a sense of Christ's presence and preaching that is clear and compassionate. People can be gathered by "branding" and "marketing," but they will gather as a crowd and not as a church. Preaching will gather the church and scatter the goats. Without that distinction everyone is confused.

"John the Baptist preached in the wilderness and all Judea and Jerusalem went out to him and were baptized by him, confessing their sins" (Mk 1:4–5).

4. THERE IS PERCEPTION (2:8)

> "When Jesus perceived in His spirit that they reasoned thus with themselves..." (2:8)

Spiritual perception is essential to leadership in the house. Without it leaders will be naive; with it they will be wise. Much suffering can be avoided with the exercise of spiritual discernment. Leaders must see the obvious and discern the hidden.

5. THERE IS POWER (2:10–11)

> "But that you may know that the Son of Man has power on earth to forgive sins"—He said to the paralytic, "I say to you, arise, take up your bed, and go to your house" (2:10–11).

When Christ is in the house, people return to their house transformed by His power. It is hard to dispute a changed life.

6. THERE IS PRAISE (2:12)

> "So that all were amazed and glorified God, saying, 'We never saw anything like this!'" (2:12).

With Jesus in the house, we will see what we have never seen before and the people will praise and glorify God who has once again honored His Son. Worship is a response to the living Christ among us.

59

The Spirit of the House
Hebrews 3:1–6

The church is God's house! The "spirit" in the house is more significant than the size, structure, or style of the house. This is more than ambiance—this is about corporate attribute.

1. THE SPIRIT OF THE "SON" OVER THE HOUSE. (3:1–2, 6)

"Therefore, holy brethren, partakers of the heavenly calling, consider the apostle and high priest of our confession, Christ Jesus, who was faithful to Him who appointed Him…" (3:1–2).

The "spirit" of the Son over His house is faithfulness.

"Unfaithfulness is one of the most outstanding sins of these days—how refreshing, then, how unspeakably blessed, to lift our eyes above the scene of ruin, and behold one who is faithful, faithful in all things, faithful at all times." **(Arthur Pink)**

2. THE SPIRIT OF THE "SERVANT" IN THE HOUSE. (3:2,6)

"Moses also was faithful in all His house" (3:2).

"Moses indeed was faithful in all His house as a servant" (3:5).

The "servant" in the house shares the spirit of the "Son" over the house. Moses faithfully followed the heavenly pattern (Heb 8:5).

"It is not great talent God blesses so much as great likeness to Jesus. A holy minister is an awful weapon in the hand of God." **(Andrew Bonar)**

"If you are faithful, you will have that honor that comes from God; His spirit will say in your hearts, well done, good and faithful servant." **(Adam Clarke)**

3. THE SPIRIT OF THE "SAINTS" IN THE HOUSE.

"Whose house we are if we hold fast the confidence and the rejoicing of hope firm to the end" (3:6)

Holding fast, confident, rejoicing, and firm to the end are all characteristics of the faithful. The servant of the house imparts the spirit of the Son to the saints within the house.

"Faithfulness and truth are the most sacred excellence and endowments of the human." **(Marcus Cicero)**

"Command those that govern your house before all your household that they keep careful watch that all your household, within and without, be faithful, painstaking, chaste, clean, honest and perfect." **(Robert Grosseteste)**

Faithfulness is the spirit of God's house. Faithfulness is the spirit in all of God's house.

60

Preparation for Visitation
Luke 3:1–18

The voice of one crying in the wilderness: "Prepare the way of the Lord..." (3:4).

John prepared a generation for visitation. The key preparation for visitation is "repentance." There are seven truths in our text concerning repentance.

1. REPENTANCE REQUIRES A VOICE. (3:3,8)

John was a voice calling for repentance in his generation. Another generation is in desperate need of voices calling for repentance. "And he went into all the region around the Jordan, preaching a baptism of repentance for the remission of sins" (3:3). "Therefore bear fruits worthy of repentance..." (3:8).

2. REPENTANCE IS PREPARATION FOR VISITATION. (3:4–6)

Repentance alone will prepare the people of God for visitation. Repentance prepares the way of the Lord (3:4). Repentance will remove the mountains of pride, straighten the crooked places, smooth the rough spots, and fill the valleys of compromise.

3. REPENTANCE IS ESSENTIAL TO ESCAPE WRATH. (3:7)

"Who warned you to flee from the wrath to come" (3:7). Jesus warned, "I tell you, no; but unless you repent you will all likewise perish" (Lk 13:5). Peter called the crowd gathered on Pentecost to repent and save themselves from a perverse generation (Acts 2:38–40).

4. REPENTANCE IS PERSONAL. (3:8)

John declared, "Therefore bear fruits worthy of repentance, and do not begin to say to yourselves, 'We have Abraham as our father,' for I say to you that God is able to raise up children from these stones" (3:8).

Repentance is personal. It is not a matter of legacy or lineage. It is not about what my parents have done—it concerns what I have done.

5. REPENTANCE WILL PRODUCE FRUITS. (3:8)

"Therefore, bear fruits worthy of repentance..." (3:8)

Acts 2:37–47 reveals immediate fruit produced by repentance: forgiveness, baptism, receiving the Holy Spirit, gladly receiving the word of God, commitment to a local church, fellowship, prayer, generosity, joy, and favor.

"Therefore every tree which does not bear good fruit is cut down and thrown into the fire" (3:9).

6. REPENTANCE RESULTS IN CHANGED BEHAVIOR. (3:10–14)

In response to John's message the crowd began to ask, "What shall we do then?" Three segments of society asked this question: the people (3:10–11); the tax collectors (3:12–13); and the soldiers (3:14). This question is the signal that the message is having its desired effect. The crowd at Pentecost asked the same question following Peter's sermon. "Men and brethren, what shall we do?" (Acts 2:37).

7. REPENTANCE LEADS TO A FAITH COMMITMENT TO JESUS CHRIST. (3:15–17)

John turned the crowd's speculation as to his identity into a declaration of personal faith and commitment to the person of Jesus Christ. Repentance always points one in the direction of Jesus Christ.

Conclusion: Every leader dreams of the day when God will visit his congregation. As leaders we must prepare our people for visitation.

61

The Sacrifice of Praise

The lyrics of a well-known worship chorus declares, "We bring the sacrifice of praise into the house of the Lord." What is the sacrifice of praise that we are to bring into the house of the Lord?

1. WE ARE THE SACRIFICE OF PRAISE BROUGHT INTO THE HOUSE OF THE LORD.

> "I beseech you therefore, brethren, by the mercies of God that you present your bodies a living sacrifice, holy, acceptable to God which is your reasonable service" (Rom 12:1).

> "Bind the sacrifice with cords to the horns of the altar" (Ps 118:27).

> "The lifting of my hands as the evening sacrifice" (Ps 141:2). "Let the offering be presented with a broken spirit and a contrite heart" (Ps 51:17).

2. THE FRUIT OF THE LIPS GIVING THANKS TO HIS NAME IS THE SACRIFICE OF PRAISE BROUGHT INTO THE HOUSE OF THE LORD.

"Therefore, by Him let us continually offer the sacrifice of praise to God, that is, the fruit of the lips giving thanks to His name"(Heb 13:15).

Worship is a verb, an action or activity engaged in, i.e., lifting hands. Worship is vocal, involving various volumes of singing and giving thanks (Lk 19:37–40).

3. EXCELLENCE IN SERVICE IS A SACRIFICE OF PRAISE BROUGHT INTO THE HOUSE OF THE LORD.

"And whatever you do, do it heartily, as to the Lord and not to men, knowing that from the Lord you will receive the reward of the inheritance for your service to the Lord Christ" (Col 3:23–24).

"I am being poured out as a drink offering on the sacrifice and service of your faith, I am glad and rejoice with you all" (Phil 2:17).

Our Father God always gives his best and asks for our best in return (Mal 1:6–14). Anything less than excellence in service to him is unacceptable. When we accept the unacceptable as acceptable we become unacceptable to him. Our best is a sacrifice of praise brought into the house of the Lord.

4. THE KINDNESS WE SHOW TO OTHERS IS A SACRIFICE OF PRAISE BROUGHT INTO THE HOUSE OF THE LORD.

"But do not forget to do good and to share, for with such sacrifice God is well pleased" (Heb 13:16).

The sacrifice of praise offered to the Lord in the previous verse (Heb 13:15) spills over into kindness toward others. Kindness manifests in "acts of kindness" and "sharing" resources with those in need (Eph 5:2).

5. THE FINANCIAL SUPPORT GIVEN TO THE LORD'S WORK IS A SACRIFICE OF PRAISE BROUGHT INTO THE HOUSE OF THE LORD.

> "Indeed, I have all and abound, I am full, having received of Epaphroditis the things sent from you, a sweet-smelling aroma, and an acceptable sacrifice well pleasing to God" (Phil 4:18).

We are most familiar with the verse that follows—(Phil 4:19). The promise of this verse is predicated on the preceding verse. We support others in love knowing God will supply our needs.

62

The Unchanging Christ

No one likes change! A rookie reporter was sent by his editor to interview one of the town's citizens who was celebrating his hundredth birthday. The reporter commented to the old gentleman, "I bet you have seen a lot of changes in your one hundred years." The old gentleman replied, "Yes sir, and I have been against every one of them." No one likes change!

There is one unchanging reality in our world. That one unchanging reality is Jesus Christ. The Old Testament declares, "For I am the Lord, I change not..." (Mal 3:6). The New Testament declares, "Jesus Christ the same yesterday, today and forever" (Heb 13:8). Christ is self-existent, eternal, and perfect. He sustains all, but is Himself independent of all. He gives to all, but is enriched by none. He has never evolved, improved, or grown. He is perfect always.

The unchanging nature of Christ benefits you and me in at least four ways:

1. HE IS REAL.

Because Christ is always the same, He is always his authentic self no matter the circumstances or the generation. People change; Christ remains the same. You never have to wonder how He will react or respond—He is the same, therefore He is always his authentic self and we are safe.

2. HE IS RELEVANT.

Christ has an immediate and direct bearing on every generation. Christ is never out of date; He is always relevant. The individual or generation who rejects him does so at its own peril.

The council of the Lord is forever, the plans of His heart to all generations (Ps 33:11). Every generation discovers Christ to be real and relevant.

3. HE IS RELIABLE.

Because Christ is always the same, He is reliable. He will never fail, harm, or disappoint. Humans fail, harm, and disappoint, but not Jesus Christ. He is totally reliable.

> "Not a word failed of any good thing which the Lord had spoken, all came to pass" (Josh 21:45).

4. HE IS RELATIONAL.

Christ can be known. He makes Himself known, therefore He can be known. Christ is relational; He connects with people (1 Jn 1:1–4).

> "I am the good shepherd; and I know my sheep, and I am known by my own" (Jn 10:14).

When **Lloyd Douglas**, author of *The Robe*, was a university student he lived in a boarding house, says **Maxine Dunnam** in

Jesus' Claim—Our Promises. Downstairs on the first floor lived an elderly retired music teacher, now infirm and unable to leave his apartment.

Douglas said that every morning they had a ritual that they would go through together. He would come down the steps, open the old man's door and ask, "Well, what's the good news?"

The old man would pick up his tuning fork, tap it on the side of his wheelchair, and say, "That's middle C! It was middle C yesterday; it will be middle C tomorrow; it will be middle C a thousand years from now. The tenor upstairs sings flat, the piano across the hall is out of tune, but my friend, that is middle C!"

The old man had discovered one thing upon which he could depend, one constant reality in his life, one "still point in a turning world." For Christians, the one "still point in a turning world," the one absolute of which there is no shadow of turning, is Jesus Christ. **Trust Him.**

63

When You're in a Hurry and God Isn't
Psalm 70:1–5

The outstanding characteristics of the great New England preacher
Phillips Brooks were poise and imperturbability. His friends,
however, knew that at times he suffered moments of frustration
and irritability. One day a friend saw him pacing the floor like a
caged lion. "What's the trouble, Dr. Brooks?" asked the friend.
"The trouble is that I am in a hurry, but God isn't."

Four times in five verses David tells God to hurry. Make haste—to
deliver (70:1). Make haste—to help (70:1). Make haste—I am poor
and needy (70:5). Make no delay—you're my help (70:5). The
inscription of this Psalm is "a Psalm to bring to remembrance."
When we get in a hurry and God isn't, there are certain things we
need to remember.

1. GOD'S WAYS ARE NOT OUR WAYS.

> "For my thoughts are not your thoughts. Nor are your ways
> my ways, says the Lord, for as the heavens are higher than
> the earth, so are my ways higher than your ways, and my

thoughts than your thoughts" (Is 55:8–9).

Our knowledge is limited and finite—God's knowledge is unlimited and infinite. We are human, He divine. God's thoughts include all the variables—ours only a few. He knows the end from the beginning—we often haven't a clue. Our prayer should be:

> "Teach me your way, O Lord, I will walk in your truth, unite my heart to fear your name" (Ps 86:11).

2. GOD'S TIMES ARE NOT OUR TIMES.

> "To everything there is a season, a time for every purpose under Heaven" (Eccl 3:1).

Timing is crucial. God's timing is always accurate. God's timing will often test us. God's delay is not His denial.

What To Do When Waiting for God's Timing

Be patient—Mistakes are made when we become impatient, e.g., Saul. We often make decisions we later regret when driven by impatience.

Be prayerful—We can often get so busy figuring out what to do that we fail to pray.

Be positive—"Do all things without complaining and disputing" (Phil 2:14).

Be productive—We should not sit by with idle folded hands during periods of waiting for God's timing. Do something while you wait.

3. GOD WORKS FOR A HIGHER PURPOSE.

The higher purpose God has for each of his children is that they be conformed to the image of His son (Rom 8:28–29). All things in life work to achieve conformity to Christ. When you know God's purpose and embrace it as your own, then you can embrace all of life rather than resisting the very thing designed to accomplish God's higher purpose.

God's "ways" and "timing" can be seen more as a source of irritation than conformity. God's higher purposes must be embraced rather than resisted. Remember: "It is God who works in you both to will and to do of His good pleasure" (Phil 2:13).

IT MAY BE A TEST!

When God is silent

When God is slow

When God is still

When we are suffering

Pass the test—promotion follows

64

The Mind of a Champion
Philippians 3:1–21

It takes more than physical strength to be a champion. Champions have a mental toughness that gives them the edge in competition. A mental toughness is required in Christian service as well as athletics. The apostle Paul demonstrated a mental toughness that enabled him to be a champion for Christ. He gives the three ingredients that produced the mind of a champion in him.

1. HE COUNTED "GAINS" NOT "LOSSES." (3:7–11)

> "Yet indeed I also count all things loss for the excellence of the knowledge of Christ Jesus my lord, for whom I have suffered the loss of all things, and count them as rubbish that I may gain Christ" (3:8).

The great apostle focused on the prize and not the price (3:8). His focus gave him a mental toughness unlike any before or since. The "little whiles of life" must not cause us to lose focus and the mental toughness to win (Jn 16:16–20; Rom 8:18).

2. HE LOOKED "BEFORE" AND NOT "BEHIND." (3:12–16)

"Brethren, I do not count myself to have apprehended; but one thing I do, forgetting those things which are behind and reaching forward to those things which are ahead" (3:13).

Champions are always stretching, growing, and reaching beyond the limits of their current achievements. For the apostle Paul, stretching was a lifestyle he embraced. Constant stretching leads to new achievements.

3. HE VIEWED LIFE FROM "ABOVE" NOT "BELOW." (3:17–21)

"For our citizenship is in Heaven, from which we also eagerly wait for the savior, the Lord Jesus Christ, who will transform our lowly body that it may be conformed to His glorious body, according to the working by which He is able even to subdue all things to Himself" (3:20–21).

Living life from an eternal perspective gives the mental toughness and spiritual stamina to prevail in all of life's challenges. The day-to-day "stuff" can be discouraging if not kept in perspective and viewed from outside the immediate circumstances.

Conclusion: There are six characteristics of mental toughness: confidence, courage, composure, enthusiasm, focus, and buoyancy.

"We must combine the toughness of the serpent with the softness of the dove. A tough mind and a tender heart." **(Dr. Martin Luther King, Jr.)**

65

The Blessing of Good Leadership

In Acts 6:1–7 "the twelve" exhibit four skills of good leadership and the blessings that result.

1. GOOD LEADERS ARE DECISIVE. (6:1–2)

> "Then the twelve summoned the multitude and said..." (6:2).

The ability to make good decisions separates leaders from followers. In decision making, it is essential to get all the facts. "When a leader has all the facts, the decision will jump out at him." **(Peter Drucker)**

"Vacillation and procrastination confuse and discourage subordinates, peers, and superiors and serve the enemy well— when you must be overly persuasive in gaining support for your decision, it's usually a sign of a bad one." **(Wess Roberts, Ph.D,** *The Leadership Secrets of Attila the Hun*)

2. GOOD LEADERS AVOID DISTRACTIONS. (6:2–4)

"It is not desirable that we should leave the word of God and serve tables, we will give ourselves continually to prayer and to the ministry of the word."

A leader's determination to avoid distractions assures the church's health and growth. Leaders know that busy doesn't mean productive.

"To be effective, leaders order their lives according to three questions: What is required? What gives the greatest return? What brings the greatest reward?" **(John Maxwell,** *21 Laws of Leadership*)

3. GOOD LEADERS DELEGATE. (6:3–4)

"Therefore, brethren, seek out among yourselves seven men…" (6:3)

If someone can do the job 80 percent as well as you, let them do it. Get out of the way, cheer them on, and make sure they get the credit. "No one will ever be a great leader who wants to do it all himself so as to get all the credit for doing it." **(Dale Carnegie)**

Delegation is based on character and competency. "Leadership in the local church should be determined by spirituality, not notoriety." **(Tony Evans)**

"The best executive is the one who has sense enough to pick good men to do what he wants done, and self-restraint enough to keep from meddling with them while they do it." **(Theodore Roosevelt)**

4. GOOD LEADERS DEVELOP PEOPLE. (6:5–6)

"Whom they set before the apostles; and when they prayed, they laid hands on them" (6:6).

To develop means: to release the possibilities, to cause to grow, to unfold, to expand, to make more valuable and effective. Leaders develop people by making emotional deposits in their lives. These deposits or impartations add value to the people and to the organization.

To continually challenge God's people is to cause frustration among the people. The leader must equip the people to develop their God-given capacity. A leader's success is not determined by how many members he has, but by how many ministers his ministry has raised up.

When a pastor primarily does the ministry in a congregation, rather than raise up leaders to perform the ministry, the growth potential of that church will usually be approximately one hundred people or less.

Conclusion: The blessing of good leadership is stated in the seventh verse of the sixth chapter of Acts. "The word of God spread, and the number of disciples multiplied in Jerusalem, and a great many of the priests were obedient to the faith."

66

The Acts 2 Church
Acts 2:40–47

The Acts 2 church is an incredible church. The key to this incredible church is its preaching. The preaching of Acts 2 produced the church of Acts 2.

THE CHURCH RISES TO THE LEVEL
OF ITS PREACHING

Quality Preaching = Quality Converts = Quality Church

You can't separate the quality of the church from its preaching. The converts of Acts 2 responded to the preaching of Acts 2. They heard the preaching, repented, received forgiveness, were baptized, received the Holy Spirit, and committed themselves to the leadership and fellowship of the church. Preaching produced these results.

Quality preaching causes the unsaved to ask the question, "What shall we do?" It was asked of John (Lk 3:10–14), of Jesus (Mk 10:17), of the apostle Paul (Acts 16:30), and of Peter (Acts 2:37).

MEDIA & PREACHING

The culture, more specifically the media of the culture, is shaping preachers and preaching.

"I believed it then, and believe now, that the profound shifts in dominant media in the last half of the twentieth century have profoundly misshapen the sensibilities of the typical American, and this in turn has led to a profound decline in preaching." **(T. David Gordon,** *Why Johnny Can't Preach***)**

If the church is to recapture her Acts 2 heritage, she must recapture the Acts 2 preaching that produced the church. The church is shaped by her preaching.

"I am told sometimes today that if a man is to be successful in preaching, he must catch the spirit of the age. Never! Our business is not to catch it, our business is to know it and correct it. In the majority of cases it needs correction rather than catching." **(G. Campbell Morgan, Quote: by David Arnold,** *60 Seconds***)**

FEED MY SHEEP

"If Jesus tests Peter's profession of love by the ministerial act of feeding his sheep, our sheep do not need gourmet meals, but they do need good, solid nourishment." **(T. David Gordon,** *Why Johnny Can't Preach)*

I am of the opinion that ministry leaders at every level need to encourage a return to passionate, God-exalting preaching. Preachers must overcome timidity and preach fearlessly.

> "The fear of man brings a snare, but whoever trusts in the Lord shall be safe" (Prov 29:25).

A fundamental law of leadership is to **"Keep the main thing the main thing."** The "main thing" in the maze of "all things" is the supremacy of preaching in producing a healthy, growing church.

> "I charge you therefore before God and the Lord Jesus Christ, who will judge the living and the dead at His appearing and His kingdom: Preach the word! Be ready in season and out of season. Convince, rebuke, exhort, with all long suffering and teaching" (2 Tim 4:1–2).

67

Try Again
Joshua 8:1–29 NLT

Israel fails miserably in their first attempt to take Ai. Their failure is twofold. The first and obvious reason is the sin of Achan. The second is Joshua's failure to inquire of the Lord. Had Joshua inquired of the Lord before launching his attack against Ai, surely he would have been told of Achan's sin and spared the nation a humiliating defeat.

Now that Achan's sin has been expiated, it's time for Joshua and Israel to try again. To assure the second attempt is successful, Joshua is given three things.

1. AN ENCOURAGING WORD.

> "Then the Lord said to Joshua, 'do not be afraid or discouraged. Take all your fighting men and attack Ai, for I have given you the king of Ai, his people, his town, and his land'" (8:1).

The word of encouragement serves to stabilize Joshua at a critical moment in the campaign. Joshua is encouraged to try again.

"A word of encouragement during a failure is worth more than a whole book of praise after a success." **(Anonymous,** *Leadership When the Heat Is On***)**

2. A WINNING STRATEGY.

"Set an ambush behind the town" (8:2b).

Following the encouragement, Joshua is given a winning strategy that will assure that Israel's recovery is complete. Joshua instructs his troops on the proper execution of the strategy, and they execute it flawlessly. The victory restores their lost confidence.

"Success is almost totally dependent upon drive and persistence. The extra energy required to make another effort or try another approach is the secret to winning." **(Dennis Waitley)**

3. AN INSPIRED TENACITY.

"Then the Lord said to Joshua, 'point the spear in your hand toward Ai, for I will hand the town over to you'" (8:18).

"The outstretched javelin in the hand of Joshua is also conceived as instrumental in effecting the victory of Israel for Joshua did not draw it back until the inhabitants of Ai were completely destroyed." **(Broadman Commentary)**

Joshua's tenacity certainly inspired his troops to recover from defeat and try again with the same tenacity demonstrated by their leader. Failure is never final or fatal unless you refuse to try again.

"A Jewish proverb says, 'There are three men who get no pity, an unsecured creditor, a henpecked husband, and a man who doesn't try again.'" **(Pulpit Commentary)**

If once you don't succeed, *TRY AGAIN.*

68

"Naïveté" Hurts the Church
Joshua 9–10 NLT

"Naïveté is a readiness to believe the claims of others without sufficient evidence." **(Merriam Webster)**

Naïveté accepts things as they appear without discernment (1Jn 4:1). Joshua and the elders of Israel demonstrate naïveté early in their attempt to conquer Canaan. The consequences of their naïveté is recorded in chapters nine and ten of the book of Joshua.

1. NAÏVETÉ LED TO DECEPTION. 9:1–15

The ruse of the Gibeonites was successful because of the naïveté of Joshua and the leaders of Israel. Joshua accepted the credibility of the Gibeonites based on appearance without any additional evidence. The decision not to properly vet the new arrivals would be a decision they would live to regret. Leaders like Solomon of old must ask for discerning hearts.

"Give me an understanding heart so that I can govern your people well and know the difference between right and wrong. For who by himself is able to govern this great people of yours?" (1Kgs 3:9 NLT).

2. NAÏVETÉ LED TO DISOBEDIENCE. 9:14–15

"So the Israelites examined their food, but they did not consult the Lord. Then Joshua made a peace treaty with them and guaranteed their safety, and the leaders of the community ratified their agreement
with a binding oath" (9:14–15 NLT).

Joshua had received specific instruction on matters of this nature. "When the Lord your God hands these nations over to you and you conquer them, you must completely destroy them. Make no treaties with them and show them no mercy" (Deut 7:2).

The naïveté of Joshua and the leaders of Israel allowed them to make decisions without inquiring of the Lord as previously directed.

"When direction from the Lord is needed, Joshua will stand before Elizar the priest, who will use the urim—one of the sacred lots cast before the Lord—to determine his will—this is how Joshua and the rest of the community of Israel will determine everything they shall do" (Num 27:21 NLT).

3. NAÏVETÉ LED TO DANGER. 10:1–13

The men of Gibeon quickly sent messengers to Joshua at his camp in Gilgal. "'Don't abandon your servants now!' they pleaded. 'Come at once.' Save us! Help us! for all the Amorite kings who live in the hill country have joined forces to attack us'" (10:6 NLT).

It wasn't long before the Gibeonites were making demands on Israel's pledge of "guaranteed safety." This pledge placed all of Israel in harm's way. Joshua and his troops marched all night to engage an enemy alliance of five kings. A battle of this magnitude could have been avoided had it not been for the naive pledge.

One of the most dramatic miracles in the Bible occurred during the battle of Israel and the Amorite kings. "The sun stood still," allowing Israel to defeat the enemy. This miracle demonstrates God's mercy and serves to warn leaders of the dangers of naïveté. The miracle was required to deliver Israel from the consequences of their leader's naive decision making.

"When you walk in God's principles, the less need you have of a miracle." **(Johnny Honaker,** Riverview, Florida)

69

How Long Are You Going to Wait?
Joshua 18:1–10 NLT

Then Joshua asked them, "How long are you going to wait before taking possession of the remaining land the Lord, the God of your ancestors, has given to you?" (18:3).

1. THERE IS A TIME TO WAIT AND A TIME TO TAKE. (18:3)

There are times when it is appropriate to wait. There is also a time when it is inappropriate to wait. There are times when we are waiting on God and times when He is waiting on us to seize what he has promised.

"To take" means to lay hold of—to take possession by force or by skill. To seize or grasp. The time for waiting is over for the people of Israel. Now is the time to take. To take full possession of what God has promised. When we take what has been given, we take lawfully.

It was not an enemy that prevented the remaining seven tribes from claiming their inheritance; it was their own indifference. To wait any longer would be sin (Jas 4:17).

2. THERE MUST BE KNOWING BEFORE GOING. (18:4)

> "Select three men from each tribe, and I will send them out to explore the land and map it out. They will return to me with a written report of their proposed divisions of their new homeland" (18:4 NLT).

You see before you seize. The surveyors were to search out the land that was to be allotted. The surveyors gathered the facts, but God gave the final guidance needed for the allotment of the land.

> "A man's heart plans his way, but the Lord directs his steps" (Prov 16:9 NKJ).

"Although we must not lean on our own understanding (Prov 3:6), we must have understanding in order for God to direct us. The more information we have the clearer God's will becomes." **(Warren Wiersbe)**

3. THE LORD MUST BE THE CENTER AND NOT PERIPHERAL. (18:1)

> "Now that the land was under Israelite control, the entire community of Israel gathered at Shiloh and set up the tabernacle" (18:1).

During Israel's travels the tabernacle was situated in the center of their camp. Three tribes camped on either side of the tabernacle. Now the tabernacle would be at the center of their land, accessible to all and a constant reminder to everyone that God was to be at the center of their life and nation.

4. LEADERS ARE LAST, BUT NOT FORGOTTEN. (19:49–50)

"After all the land was divided among the tribes, the Israelites gave a piece of land to Joshua as his allocation. For the Lord had said 'He could have any town he wanted.' He chose Timnath-Serah in the hill country of Ephraim. He rebuilt the town and lived there"
(19:49–50 NLT).

Joshua took the mountain region of Ephraim. This region would be more difficult to possess, but it was the portion Joshua chose for himself.

The leader was last to take his allotment, but take it he did. Timnath-Serah means an abundant portion—that which is left over and above. Leaders who serve God's people are assured they will receive an abundant portion for their sacrifice of service.

The promise made to the servants of God is a hundredfold in this life and in the age to come, eternal life (Mk 10:28–31).

70

Going Public with Your Faith
John 19:38–42

Joseph of Arimathea is a familiar name to believers. Joseph is identified historically with the burial of Jesus. Joseph is described in the gospel accounts as "a just man who was waiting for the kingdom of God." He was a prominent member of the Jewish Council known as the Sanhedrin. Joseph is known as "a disciple of Jesus, but secretly for fear of the Jews."

Joseph was a "closet Christian" about to go public with his faith. There are three things to observe about this reluctant witness.

1. JOSEPH TOOK A RISK. (JN 19:38)

The first thing we observe about Joseph is when he goes to Pilate and asks to be given custody of the body of Jesus.

Joseph steps from the comfort of his anonymity and goes public with his faith.

- He can be a silent, secret follower no longer.
  After receiving permission from Pilate to take custody of

Jesus's body, Joseph personally and very publicly takes the body of Jesus from the cross.

- He buries Jesus in his own tomb.
  Joseph is aware of the possible negative consequences of his very public action. However, he takes the risk. He can be secret and silent no longer (Mt 10:27–31).

2. JOSEPH TOOK COURAGE. (Mk 15:43)

"Joseph of Arimathea, a prominent council member, who was himself waiting for the Kingdom of God, coming and taking courage, went in to Pilate and asked for the body of Jesus" (15:43).

Courage is required when a risk is taken. Joseph not only "took a risk" he "took courage" equal to his risk (2 Tim 1:6–9).

"Courage is doing what you're afraid to do. There can be no courage unless you're scared." **(Eddie Richenbacker**, *Bits & Pieces*)

3. JOSEPH TOOK A FRIEND. (JN 19:39)

"And Nicodemus, who at first came to Jesus by night, also came, bringing a mixture of myrrh and aloes, about a hundred pounds" (19:39).

Courage is contagious. Joseph's courage encouraged Nicodemus to take courage and go public with his faith. Both men were members of the Jewish Sanhedrin and kept silent as to their personal faith in Jesus as the Messiah. Courage in the face of risk empowers others to be courageous. Joseph inspired Nicodemus, and together they lowered the body of Jesus from the cross (a very public act) and took him to be buried in Joseph's tomb.

The time has come for all Christ's followers to step out of the safety and comfort of their anonymity and go public with their faith. Who might be inspired by our courage in the face of risk?

71

What Faith in God Will Do
Mark 11:12–26

So Jesus answered and said to them, "Have faith in God" (11:22).

Ministry is a work of faith. God proportions faith equal to the task He assigns (Rom 12:3–8). Each minister and Christian worker can look on their assignment and say emphatically, "I have faith for this."

In our text Jesus articulates and demonstrates "What Faith in God Will Do."

1. FAITH WILL DRY UP WHAT NEEDS TO BE DRIED UP. (11:12–14, 20–21)

When Jesus encounters a fig tree having leaves and no fruit, His response illustrates that there are things that should not be allowed to continue as they are. Faith in God will dry up what needs to be dried up.

2. FAITH WILL REMOVE WHAT NEEDS TO BE REMOVED. (11:22–23)

Mountains of opposition must not be allowed to obstruct the advancement of God's kingdom on the earth (Zech 4:7–10). Faith implemented by prophetic pronouncement will remove obstacles to God's work moving forward.

3. FAITH WILL GET DONE WHAT NEEDS TO BE DONE. (11:23)

> "Believe that those things he says will be done, he will have whatever he says" (11:23).

"Whatever" needs to be done will be done in response to faith. Faith always has a voice and is not silent (2 Cor 4:13). A silent faith is an inactive faith.

"Faith has to do with things that are not seen and hope with things that are not at hand." **(Thomas Aquinas)**

4. FAITH WILL PROVIDE WHAT YOU NEED BUT DON'T HAVE. (11:24)

> "Therefore, I say, whatever things you ask when you pray, believe that you have them and you will have them" (11:24).

"Whatever things" are required for the work of ministry will be supplied in abundance when we pray and believe (2 Cor 9:8). Faith will secure what you need but don't have.

"God our father has made all things depend on faith so that whoever has faith will have everything. And whoever does not have faith will have nothing." **(Martin Luther)**

"A man lives by believing something, not by debating and arguing about many things." **(Thomas Carlyle)**

5. FAITH WILL HEAL WHAT NEEDS TO BE HEALED. (11:25–26)

> "And whenever you stand praying, if you have anything against anyone, forgive him, that your father in heaven may also forgive you your trespasses" (11:25).

Human relationships are fragile and often require healing. Forgiveness is not optional for the believer; it is required. Faith enables the believer to extend forgiveness to the offender. When confronted with the prospect of forgiving a person for repeated offenses in a single day, the disciples petitioned for an increase of faith equal to the task (Lk 17:1–5). Faith is essential in the forgiveness and healing of fractured relationships. Faith will heal what needs to be healed.

Faith is the currency of heaven. Faith gives one access to "the riches of heaven" (Phil 4:19). Faith is the hand that grasps all the promises of God.

During an especially trying time in the work of the China Inland Mission, Hudson Taylor wrote to his wife, "We have twenty five cents...and all the promises of God." **(Warren Wiersbe)**

"Faith is to believe what we do not see; and the reward of faith is to see what we believe." **(Augustine)**

72

A Leader's Resolve
Psalm 101:1–8 NLT

Jonathan Edwards, before his twentieth birthday, wrote seventy resolutions that would give shape and focus to his life. Every week for thirty-five years, Jonathan Edwards would read these resolutions.

Edwards prefaced his resolutions with these words: "Being sensible that I am unable to do anything without God's help, I do humbly entreat Him by His grace to enable me to keep these resolutions, so far as they are agreeable to His will, for Christ's sake."

Great leaders have great resolve! To be "resolved" is to have a firm and fixed purpose. David demonstrates great resolve in many of his psalms. In our text no fewer than twelve times in eight verses does David state his resolve with the words "I will." A leader's strength comes from the leader's resolve. Without "resolve" the leader will flounder.

1. I RESOLVE TO WORSHIP.

"I will sing of your love and justice, Lord. I will praise you with song" (101:1).

2. I RESOLVE TO LIVE ABOVE REPROACH.

"I will be careful to live a blameless life—when will you come to help me?" (101:2a).

3. I RESOLVE TO LIVE WITH INTEGRITY IN MY PRIVATE LIFE.

"I will lead a life of integrity in my own home" (101:2b).

4. I RESOLVE TO ELIMINATE THE VILE AND VULGAR FROM MY LIFE.

"I will refuse to look on anything vile or vulgar" (101:3a).

5. I RESOLVE TO HAVE NO DEALINGS WITH CROOKED MEN, NOR WILL I EMBRACE THEIR WAYS.

"I hate all who deal crookedly; I will have nothing to do with them" (101:3b).

6. I RESOLVE TO HOLD FAST TO WHAT IS TRUE AND REFUSE TO FELLOWSHIP WITH THE UNFAITHFUL.

"I will reject perverse ideas and stay away from every evil" (101:4).

7. I RESOLVE TO AVOID HYPOCRISY IN RELATIONSHIPS.

"I will not tolerate people who slander their neighbors..." (101:5a).

8. I RESOLVE TO HAVE NO FELLOWSHIP WITH THE CONCEITED AND ARROGANT.

"He who has a haughty look and a proud and arrogant heart I cannot and will not tolerate" (101:5b).

9. I RESOLVE TO SURROUND MYSELF WITH FAITHFUL PEOPLE.

"I will search for faithful people to be my companions..." (101:6a).

10. I RESOLVE THAT ONLY THOSE ABOVE REPROACH WILL SERVE ME.

"Only those above reproach will be allowed to serve me" (101:6b).

11. I RESOLVE TO EMPLOY ONLY THE TRUTHFUL AND TRUSTWORTHY.

"I will not allow deceivers to serve in my house, and liars will not stay in my presence" (101:7).

12. I RESOLVE DAILY TO REMOVE THE INFLUENCE OF EVIL THAT GOD'S WORK MAY PROSPER.

"My daily task will be to ferret out the wicked and free the city of the Lord from their grip" (101:8).

"Unlike David, we do not have authority to execute judgment on the wicked, but if our hearts and homes are what God wants them to be, our influence will be felt in the city and the nation." (**Warren Wiersbe**, *With the Word*)

"Strength is a matter of a made-up mind." (**John Beecher**)

CONTACT INFORMATION

Frank P. Adams

27 Dawson Drive
Fredericksburg, VA. 22405
540-374-0507

www.newlevelchurchconsulting.com

frankpadams@verizon.net

Made in the USA
Lexington, KY
22 September 2015